PRAYERS ACROSS THE CENTURIES

PRAYERS
ACROSS THE
CENTURIES

ABRAHAM

JESUS

ST. AUGUSTINE

MARTIN LUTHER

SUSANNA WESLEY

Harold Shaw Publishers
Wheaton, Illinois

Copyright © 1993 by Harold Shaw Publishers

Vinita Hampton Wright, editor

ISBN 0-87788-646-6

Library of Congress Cataloging-in-Publication Data

Prayers across the centuries / Vinita Hampton Wright, editor.
    p. cm.
  Includes index.
  ISBN 0-87788-646-6
  1. Prayers. I. Wright, Vinita Hampton, 1958-   .
BV245.P8155 1993
242'.8—dc20   92-32268
                                              CIP

---

99 98 97 96 95 94

10 9 8 7 6 5 4 3 2

CONTENTS

Lord Jesus Christ,
Son of God,
have mercy upon me.

*—the "Jesus Prayer,"
from 6th-7th centuries*

Introduction

Prayers Across the Centuries is more than a collection of prayers; it is a family album containing remnants from the lives of God's people through ages of struggle, victory, desire, and exultation. In its opening pages we hear the prayers of Abraham and Daniel, Hannah, and Jeremiah—those faithful ones who conversed with God before they even knew of the coming Jesus, in whose name future believers would pray. Later come the praises and requests of Mary, Jesus, the apostle Paul, and others of New Testament times whose words became the basis of Christian theology.

The persecuted church, martyred saints, isolated monks, Christian writers and thinkers add their words to the story of prayer through the early and Middle Ages, when printed prayers were a rare treasure, and few people had the ability to read them. As the decades progress, God's family expands and the variety of prayers increases. We hear the longings of bishops and kings, missionaries and hymnwriters, poets, mothers, evangelists, and modern saints. Some prayers were said by famous people. Others can no longer be traced to their sources; they are merely a part of our long and colorful story—this story of conversation between God and his children.

This collection does not begin to be comprehensive or even representative of the worldwide church's prayer life. Research was limited mainly to English language sources, leaving out volumes of devotional materials from countries outside the Western hemisphere. Many more men than women appear in the attributions. Traditionally, the education of women has been neglected, and they were often unable to record their devotions. Women have long been mighty, diligent, and passionate at prayer; it is a great loss to the world that this part of the church's history has not survived.

These prayers can be used as devotions, for leisure reading, or as a general resource. Whatever the occasion, their
words will powerfully enrich and broaden the experience
of faith.

*Note to reader: For the purpose of easier reading, all pronouns
have been modernized (Thee/you) and some words of an older
English style have been changed (gavest/gave). In rare cases,
entire phrases and sentences have been altered for better understanding; these are indicated by the word "adapted" in the at-
tribution.*

PRAYERS
OF THE
BIBLE

Introduction

It is surprising to discover just how many prayers are in the Bible and how wide their variety. We are familiar with the famous ones, like Mary's Magnificat and the Lord's Prayer. But in the scope of Scripture we find the prayers of prophets, poets, and military leaders, childless women and people under seige. They do not mince words. They cry out to God for mercy, for help and justice. Their gratitude and praise resound during times of victory and prosperity.

There is a common denominator to all their prayers. Somehow these people understood that their lives were not solely in their own hands. They recognized the God who created the world, scrutinized it, and took active part in its happenings. They saw this God alternately as Righteous Judge, Caregiver, and Ruler of the elements. A few people of Old Testament times, such as the psalmist David, had the insight to know that the All-Powerful could also be gentle as a shepherd. Not until the coming of Jesus of Nazareth did anyone dare to call God "Abba," a child's trusting reference to his father.

In the book of Hebrews, the criteria for effective prayer is put simply: "And without faith, it is impossible to please God, because anyone who comes to him must believe that he exists and that he rewards those who earnestly seek him" (11:6). We are prone to think that real faith is the assurance that God will do what we ask. However, the people whose prayers are recorded in the Book of books often possessed only the most basic faith; they believed that God *was* and that if they sought him out with genuine hearts, *they would be heard.*

Note: Some prayers span entire chapters of the Bible. In order to include a wider selection of prayers, some have been shortened by omitting verses. This is indicated in the chapter and verse references and by ellipses in the quoted text.

Prayers in Ancient Jewish History

The Lord has just told Abraham that he will destroy the city of Sodom for its wickedness. Abraham pleads for the city:

> Will you sweep away the righteous with the wicked? What if there are fifty righteous people in the city? Will you really sweep it away and not spare the place for the sake of the fifty righteous people in it? Far be it from you to do such a thing—to kill the righteous with the wicked, treating the righteous and the wicked alike. Far be it from you! Will not the Judge of all the earth do right? . . . May the Lord not be angry, but let me speak just once more. What if only ten can be found there?
> —*Genesis 18:23-25, 32*

Shortly before Isaac's death, he blesses his son Jacob, praying these words for him:

> May God give you of the dew of heaven,
>   and of the fatness of the earth,
>   and plenty of grain and wine.
> Let peoples serve you,
>   and nations bow down to you.
> Be lord over your brothers,
>   and may your mother's sons bow down to you.

Cursed be every one who curses you,
   and blessed be every one who blesses you!
—*Genesis 27:28-29 (RSV)*

And Jacob's blessing to his son, Joseph, and Joseph's sons:

God, before whom my fathers
Abraham and Isaac did walk,
the God which fed me
all my life long unto this day,
The Angel which redeemed me from all evil,
bless the lads; and let my name be named on them,
and the name of my fathers Abraham and Isaac;
and let them grow into a multitude
in the midst of the earth.
—*Genesis 48:15-16 (KJV)*

*The leader Moses has just witnessed the miraculous escape of the
Hebrew people from the Egyptians. In one of the most famous
incidents of Bible history, God parted the waters of the Red Sea;
Moses and his people walked across on dry ground, but when the
Egyptian armies thundered after, the waters fell back as they
were, drowning the pursuers. Here is the song of thanksgiving
Moses offers to God after this event.*

I will sing to the LORD,
   for he is highly exalted.
The horse and its rider
   he has hurled into the sea.
The LORD is my strength and my song;
   he has become my salvation.
He is my God, and I will praise him,

my father's God, and I will exalt him.
The LORD is a warrior;
  the LORD is his name. . . .
Your right hand, O LORD,
  was majestic in power.
Your right hand, O LORD,
  shattered the enemy.
In the greatness of your majesty
  you threw down those who opposed you.
You unleashed your burning anger;
  it consumed them like stubble.
By the blast of your nostrils
  the waters piled up.
The surging waters stood firm like a wall;
  the deep waters congealed in the
  heart of the sea. . . .
Who among the gods is like you,
  O LORD?
Who is like you—
  majestic in holiness,
  awesome in glory,
  working wonders?
You stretched out your right hand
  and the earth swallowed them.
In your unfailing love you will lead
  the people you have redeemed.
In your strength you will guide them
  to your holy dwelling.
The nations will hear and tremble . . .
You will bring [your people] in and plant them
  on the mountain of your inheritance—

the place, O LORD, you made for your dwelling,
the sanctuary, O Lord, your hands established.
The LORD will reign
for ever and ever.
—*Exodus 15:1-3, 6-8, 11-14, 17-18*

---

*What a special privilege, to have God himself tell you how to
pray for the people under your care! Here is the blessing the
LORD instructed Israel's priests (Aaron and his sons) to pray
over the nation:*

The LORD bless you and keep you;
The LORD make his face to shine upon you, and be
gracious to you;
The LORD lift up his countenance upon you, and
give you peace.
—*Numbers 6:24-26 (RSV)*

---

*For years Hannah was childless. Her torment increased as her
husband's other wife was blessed with children. One year, Hannah went to the temple and poured out her heart to God, promis-
ing that if she had a child, she would dedicate him to God's
service. Her longing has now become reality. Here is Hannah's
prayer of thanksgiving after a long and arduous wait for mother-
hood:*

My heart rejoices in the LORD;
in the LORD my horn is lifted high.
My mouth boasts over my enemies,
for I delight in your deliverance.
There is no one holy like the LORD;
there is no one besides you;
there is no Rock like our God. . . .

Do not keep talking so proudly
  or let your mouth speak such arrogance,
  for the LORD is a God who knows,
  and by him deeds are weighed.
The bows of the warriors are broken,
  but those who stumbled are armed with strength.
Those who were full hire themselves out for food,
  but those who were hungry hunger no more.
She who was barren has borne seven children,
  but she who has had many sons pines away.
The LORD brings death and makes alive;
  he brings down to the grave and raises up.
The LORD sends poverty and wealth;
  he humbles and he exalts.
He raises the poor from the dust
  and lifts the needy from the ash heap;
  he seats them with princes
  and has them inherit a throne of honor.
For the foundations of the earth are the LORD's;
  upon them he has set the world.
He will guard the feet of his saints,
  but the wicked will be silenced in darkness.
It is not by strength that one prevails;
  those who oppose the LORD will be shattered.
He will thunder against them from heaven;
  the LORD will judge the ends of the earth.
He will give strength to his king
  and exalt the horn of his anointed.
—*1 Samuel 2:1–10*

King David has just heard from Nathan the prophet that God will go with him and his nation. David's response:

> O Lord God, why have you showered your bless-
> ings on such an insignificant person as I am? And
> now, in addition to everything else, you speak of
> giving me an eternal dynasty! Such generosity is
> far beyond any human standard! Oh, Lord God! . . .
>
> How great you are, Lord God! We have never
> heard of any other god like you. And there is no
> other god. What other nation in all the earth has
> received such blessings as Israel, your people? For
> you have rescued your chosen nation in order to
> bring glory to your name. You have done great
> miracles to destroy Egypt and its gods. You chose
> Israel to be your people forever, and you became
> our God.
>
> And now, Lord God, do as you have promised
> concerning me and my family. And may you be
> eternally honored when you have established Israel
> as your people and have established my dynasty
> before you.
>
> —*2 Samuel 7:18-19, 22-26 (TLB)*

If God were to say to you, "Whatever you ask for, I'll give you," what would you ask for? This is what happened to Solomon, son of David and successor to the throne. And Solomon made a very wise request:

> You were wonderfully kind to my father David
> because he was honest and true and faithful to you,
> and obeyed your commands. And you have con-

tinued your kindness to him by giving him a son to succeed him. O Lord my God, now you have made me the king instead of my father David, but I am as a little child who doesn't know his way around. And here I am among your own chosen people, a nation so great that there are almost too many people to count! Give me an understanding mind so that I can govern your people well and know the difference between what is right and what is wrong. For who by himself is able to carry such a heavy responsibility?
—*1 Kings 3:6-9 (TLB)*

King David has taken up a free-will collection for the building of the temple. So much is given by the people that he must instruct them not to give any more. Here is David's response to their generosity:

. . . Everything comes from you, and we have given you only what comes from your hand. We are aliens and strangers in your sight, as were all our forefathers. Our days on earth are like a shadow, without hope. O LORD our God, as for all this abundance that we have provided for building you a temple for your Holy Name, it comes from your hand, and all of it belongs to you.

I know, my God, that you test the heart and are pleased with integrity. All these things have I given willingly and with honest intent. And now I have seen with joy how willingly your people who are here have given to you. O LORD, God of our fathers, Abraham, Isaac and Israel, keep this desire in the

hearts of your people forever, and keep their hearts loyal to you.
—*1 Chronicles 29:14-18*

After generations of worshiping in a moveable tabernacle, the people of Israel finally have a temple, built to the Lord's specifications. As the people gather to dedicate the temple, King Solomon offers up this prayer:

O LORD, God of Israel, there is no God like you in heaven or on earth—you who keep your covenant of love with your servants who continue wholeheartedly in your way. You have kept your promise to your servant David my father; with your mouth you have promised and with your hand you have fulfilled it—as it is today . . . And now, O LORD, God of Israel, let your word that you promised your servant David come true. But will God really dwell on earth with men? The heavens, even the highest heavens, cannot contain you. How much less this temple I have built! Yet give attention to your servant's prayer and his plea for mercy, O LORD my God. Hear the cry and the prayer that your servant is praying in your presence. May your eyes be open toward this temple day and night, this place of which you said you would put your Name there. May you hear the prayer your servant prays toward this place. Hear the supplications of your servant and of your people Israel when they pray toward this place. Hear from heaven, your dwelling place; and when you hear, forgive.
—*2 Chronicles 6:14-15, 17-21*

It is one of the most renowned of Old Testament stories. In a land full of false gods and idol worship, Elijah the prophet challenges the priests of Baal to a contest. Whoever's god sends down fire to consume the offering is the true God. Baal's priests pray loud and long, gashing themselves and screaming toward heaven, but no fire comes. Finally, Elijah summons the Lord God with this simple prayer:

> O LORD, God of Abraham, Isaac and Israel, let it be known today that you are God in Israel and that I am your servant and have done all these things at your command. Answer me, O LORD, answer me, so these people will know that you, O LORD, are God, and that you are turning their hearts back again.
> —*1 Kings 18:36-37*

God sends down fire enough to consume the offering and lap up the water all around it. Elijah has the false priests killed. It is a day of great victory. But soon Elijah hears that Queen Jezebel has planned to kill him, so he flees to the desert. There he prays:

> I've had enough . . . Take away my life. I've got to die sometime, and it might as well be now . . . I have been working very hard for the Lord God of the armies of heaven, but the people have broken their covenant and have torn down your altars; they have killed every one of your prophets except me; and now they are trying to kill me, too.
> —*1 Kings 19:4, 14 (TLB)*

In the end, God shows Elijah that he is not so alone as he thinks. Elijah comes out of his depression and goes on to serve the Lord.

Ezra was a teacher of the Law, appointed to set up judges throughout the new settlement of Hebrews who were returning from exile. He was to teach the Law to all and administer justice. He found the people in a poor state when he arrived—a remnant of God's nation that had forgotten his law and his ways:

O my God, I am too ashamed and disgraced to lift up my face to you, my God, because our sins are higher than our heads and our guilt has reached to the heavens. From the days of our forefathers until now, our guilt has been great. Because of our sins, we and our kings and our priests have been subjected to the sword and captivity, to pillage and humiliation at the hand of foreign kings, as it is today.

But now, for a brief moment, the LORD our God has been gracious in leaving us a remnant and giving us a firm place in his sanctuary, and so our God gives light to our eyes and a little relief in our bondage. Though we are slaves, our God has not deserted us in our bondage. He has shown us kindness in the sight of the kings of Persia: He has granted us new life to rebuild the house of our God and repair its ruins, and he has given us a wall of protection in Judah and Jerusalem. . . .

What has happened to us is a result of our evil deeds and our great guilt, and yet, our God, you have punished us less than our sins have deserved . . . O LORD, God of Israel, you are righteous! We are left this day as a remnant. Here we are before you in our guilt, though because of it not one of us can stand in your presence.

—*Ezra 9:6-9, 13, 15*

Most people have heard the story of Job. Although he was a righteous man, pain and desolation came crashing into his life without any apparent reason. In the beginning Job was able to praise God and "keep a stiff upper lip," but eventually his frustration comes to the surface, as is clear in this prayer:

> Your hands fashioned and made me;
>   and now you turn and destroy me. . . .
> If I am wicked, woe to me!
> If I am righteous, I cannot lift up my head,
>   for I am filled with disgrace
>   and look upon my affliction . . .
> Are not the days of my life few?
> Let me alone, that I may find a little comfort
>   before I go, never to return,
>   to the land of gloom and deep darkness,
>   the land of gloom and chaos,
>   where light is like darkness.
> —*Job 10:8, 15, 20-22 (NRSVB)*

After God speaks to Job, the man is ashamed of the accusations he made at a holy God.

> I know that you can do all things;
>   no plan of yours can be thwarted.
> You asked, "Who is this that obscures
>   my counsel without knowledge?"
> Surely I spoke of things I did not understand,
>   things too wonderful for me to know.
> You said, "Listen now, and I will speak;
>   I will question you, and you shall answer me."
> My ears had heard of you

but now my eyes have seen you.
Therefore I despise myself and repent in dust
   and ashes.
—*Job 42:2-6*

---

*Some of the most wrenching prayers are voiced by the prophets
of God—people who could see the truth more clearly than others
and who longed for peace, godliness, justice, and prosperity to
return to a wrecked nation. Like most people, these prophets were
not always patient with God's timetable. In the following prayers
we hear the desperate cries of Isaiah, Jeremiah, Daniel, and
Habakkuk.*

Oh, that you would rend the heavens and
   come down,
      that the mountains would tremble before you!
   . . . You come to the help of those who gladly
   do right,
      who remember your ways.
But when we continued to sin against them,
   you were angry.
How then can we be saved?
All of us have become like one who is unclean,
   and all our righteous acts are like filthy rags;
   we all shrivel up like a leaf,
   and like the wind our sins sweep us away,
No one calls on your name
   or strives to lay hold of you;
      for you have hidden your face from us
      and made us waste away because of our sins.
Yet, O LORD, you are our Father.
We are the clay, you are the potter;

we are all the work of your hand.
Do not be angry beyond measure, O Lord;
   do not remember our sins forever.
Oh, look upon us, we pray,
   for we are all your people.
Your sacred cities have become a desert;
   even Zion is a desert, Jerusalem a desolation.
Our holy and glorious temple,
   where our fathers praised you,
   has been burned with fire,
   and all that we treasured lies in ruins.
After all this, O Lord, will you hold yourself back?
Will you keep silent and punish us beyond
   measure?
—*Isaiah 64:1, 5-12*

O Lord, I know it is not within the power of man to
map his life and plan his course—so you correct
me, Lord; but please be gentle. Don't do it in your
anger, for I would die. Pour out your fury on the
nations who don't obey the Lord, for they have
destroyed Israel and made a wasteland of this entire country.
—*Jeremiah 10:23-25 (TLB)*

Remember, O Lord, what has happened to us;
   look, and see our disgrace.
Our inheritance has been turned over to aliens,
   our homes to foreigners.

We have become orphans and fatherless,
    our mothers like widows.
We must buy the water we drink;
    our wood can be had only at a price. . . .
Joy is gone from our hearts;
    our dancing has turned to mourning.
The crown has fallen from our head.
Woe to us, for we have sinned!
Because of this our hearts are faint,
    because of these things our eyes grow dim
    for Mount Zion, which lies desolate,
    with jackals prowling over it.
You, O LORD, reign forever;
    your throne endures from
    generation to generation.
Why do you always forget us?
Why do you forsake us so long?
Restore us to yourself, O LORD, that we may return;
    renew our days as of old
    unless you have utterly rejected us
    and are angry with us beyond measure.
—*Lamentations 5:1-4, 15-22*

Our sins and the iniquities of our fathers have
made Jerusalem and your people an object of scorn
to all those around us. Now, our God, hear the
prayer and petitions of your servant. For your sake,
O Lord, look with favor on your desolate sanctuary. Give ear, O God, and hear, open your eyes
and see the desolation of the city that bears your

Name. We do not make requests of you because we are righteous, but because of your great mercy. O Lord, listen! O Lord, forgive! O Lord, hear and act! For your sake, O my God, do not delay, because your city and your people bear your Name.
—*Daniel 9:16-19*

O Lord, how long must I call for help before you will listen? I shout to you in vain; there is no answer. "Help! Murder!" I cry, but no one comes to save. Must I forever see this sin and sadness all around me?

Wherever I look there is oppression and bribery and men who love to argue and to fight. The law is not enforced and there is no justice given in the courts, for the wicked far outnumber the righteous, and bribes and trickery prevail.
—*Habakkuk 1:2-4 (TLB)*

Though the fig tree does not bud
and there are no grapes on the vines,
though the olive crop fails
and the fields produce no food,
though there are no sheep in the pen
and no cattle in the stalls,
yet I will rejoice in the LORD,
I will be joyful in God my Savior.
—*Habakkuk 3:17-18*

Imagine being a captive in a foreign country—a refugee with an unrecognized religion and culture, and no rights. Yet you are the only person in the entire country with the ability to interpret the disturbing dreams of the ruling monarch. Such was Daniel's position in Babylon. King Nebuchadnezzar was so distraught over the failure of his own interpreters and wise men that he had had them executed. Enter Daniel, a young Hebrew refugee. As he stood before Nebuchadnezzar, and just before delivering the meaning of the king's dreams, here is the prayer Daniel uttered:

> Praise be to the name of God for ever and ever;
>> wisdom and power are his.
> He changes times and seasons;
>> he sets up kings and deposes them.
> He gives wisdom to the wise
>> and knowledge to the discerning.
> He reveals deep and hidden things;
>> he knows what lies in darkness,
>> and light dwells with him.
> I thank and praise you, O God of my fathers:
> You have given me wisdom and power,
>> you have made known to me what we asked
>> of you,
>> you have made known to us the dream of
>> the king.
> —*Daniel 2:20-23*

Most people have heard of Jonah, the prophet who ran from his duties and was subsequently thrown into the sea and swallowed by a great fish. Here is Jonah, praying inside the fish:

> You hurled me into the deep,
>> into the very heart of the seas,

and the currents swirled about me;
all your waves and breakers swept over me.
I said, "I have been banished from your sight;
yet I will look again toward your holy temple."
The engulfing waters threatened me,
the deep surrounded me;
seaweed was wrapped around my head.
To the roots of the mountains I sank down;
the earth beneath barred me in forever.
But you brought my life up from the pit,
O Lord my God.
When my life was ebbing away,
I remembered you, Lord,
and my prayer rose to you,
to your holy temple.
Those who cling to worthless idols
forfeit the grace that could be theirs.
But I, with a song of thanksgiving,
will sacrifice to you.
What I have vowed I will make good.
Salvation comes from the Lord.
—*Jonah 2:3-9*

*It has been a few hundred years since a prophet has spoken God's
message to Israel. The people's hopes for a promised Messiah
grow weak with time. Then an angel visits a young village girl
named Mary, and tells her that she is pregnant with God's Son.
His name will be Jesus, and he will save his people from their
sins. The virgin's response has been sung and spoken the world
over ever since, especially during Christmastide:*

My soul magnifies the Lord,

and my spirit rejoices in God my Savior,
>   for he has regarded the low estate of his
>   handmaiden.
> For behold, henceforth all generations will call
>   me blessed;
>   for he who is mighty has done great things for me,
>   and holy is his name.
> And his mercy is on those who fear him
>   from generation to generation.
> He has shown strength with his arm,
>   he has scattered the proud in the imagination of
>   their hearts,
>   he has put down the mighty from their thrones,
>   and exalted those of low degree;
>   he has filled the hungry with good things,
>   and the rich he has sent empty away.
> He has helped his servant Israel,
>   in remembrance of his mercy,
>   as he spoke to our fathers,
>   to Abraham and to his posterity for ever.
> —*Luke 1:46-55* (RSV)

The old man Simeon has been told by the Holy Spirit that he will see the Savior before he dies. His prayer as he holds the baby Jesus in his arms:

Sovereign Lord, as you have promised,
>   you now dismiss your servant in peace.
> For my eyes have seen your salvation,
>   which you have prepared in the sight of

all people,
a light for revelation to the Gentiles
and for glory to your people Israel.
—*Luke 2:29-32*

The Prayers of Jesus and the Book of Psalms

The disciples of Jesus have been observing him for some time now; they have witnessed his miracles and sat under his teaching. They have also noticed that he goes off by himself frequently to pray. The disciples no doubt have prayers from their Jewish heritage catalogued in their memories—recitations learned from early childhood. But what must this man be saying to God, day after day, in order to receive such power and wisdom?

At last they ask him, "Lord, teach us to pray." His example mixes concern for daily physical needs with protection from evil, concerns about relationships with others along with the individual's standing with God. The "Lord's Prayer" is repeated in more places and situations worldwide than any other passage of Holy Scripture.

> Our Father in heaven,
> hallowed be your name,
> your kingdom come,
> your will be done
> on earth as it is in heaven.
> Give us today our daily bread.
> Forgive us our debts,
> as we also have forgiven our debtors.
> And lead us not into temptation,
> but deliver us from the evil one.
> —*Matthew 6:9-13*

There really are not many of Jesus' prayers recorded—probably because he often sought God's guidance in solitude. He didn't keep a journal or have a secretary to preserve his words. But the few words passed down to us say much about the Son of God. For example, what he said just before he raised Lazarus from the dead:

Father, I thank you that you have heard me. I knew that you always hear me, but I said this for the benefit of the people standing here, that they may believe that you sent me.
—*John 11:41-42*

—his words in the Garden of Gethsemane before he would be seized by the officials and taken to trial:

Abba, Father . . . everything is possible for you. Take this cup from me. Yet not what I will, but what you will.
—*Mark 14:36*

—what he prayed for those who tortured and crucified him:

Father, forgive them, for they know not what they do.
—*Luke 23:34 (KJV)*

—the agony he voiced while the weight of the world's sin was upon him:

My God, my God, why have you forsaken me?
—*Mark 15:34*

—and his dying words:

> Father, into your hands I commit my spirit.
> **—Luke 23:46**

The lengthiest recorded prayer of Jesus Christ is contained in the 17th chapter of the Gospel of John. He has just spoken frankly with his followers about what is to come. Then, in their presence, he prays for himself, for the disciples, and for future believers. Here are segments of those crucial and poignant words to the heavenly Father.

—for himself:

> Father, the time has come. Glorify your Son, that your Son may glorify you. For you granted him authority over all people that he might give eternal life to all those you have given him. Now this is eternal life: that they may know you, the only true God, and Jesus Christ, whom you have sent. I have brought you glory on earth by completing the work you gave me to do. And now, Father, glorify me in your presence with the glory I had with you before the world began.
> **—John 17:1-5**

—for his followers:

> I have revealed you to those whom you gave me out of the world. They were yours; you gave them to me and they have obeyed your word. . . . They knew with certainty that I came from you, and they believed that you sent me. I pray for them. I am not

praying for the world, but for those you have given me, for they are yours. All I have is yours, and all you have is mine. And glory has come to me through them. I will remain in the world no longer, but they are still in the world, and I am coming to you. Holy Father, protect them by the power of your name—the name you gave me—so that they may be one as we are one. . . . I say these things while I am still in the world, so that they may have the full measure of my joy within them. My prayer is not that you take them out of the world but that you protect them from the evil one. They are not of the world, even as I am not of it. Sanctify them by the truth; your word is truth. As you sent me into the world, I have sent them into the world.
—*John 17:6, 8-11, 13, 15-18*

—and for all believers to come:

My prayer is not for them alone. I pray also for those who will believe in me through their message, that all of them may be one, Father, just as you are in me and I am in you. May they also be in us so that the world may believe that you have sent me. I have given them the glory that you gave me, that they may be one as we are one: I in them and you in me. May they be brought to complete unity to let the world know that you sent me and have loved them even as you have loved me.
—*John 17:20-23*

The book of Psalms is primarily a book of prayer. In it, poets, military men, musicians, kings, and shepherds lay bare what is on their hearts. Praise, anger, disappointment, joy, thanksgiving, and cries for help all issue from this tremendous prayer book. Following are some of the most well-known and often-repeated selections.

O LORD, how many are my foes!
Many are rising against me;
   many are saying of me,
   there is no help for him in God.
But thou, O LORD, art a shield about me,
   my glory, and the lifter of my head.
I cry aloud to the LORD,
   and he answers me from his holy hill.
I lie down and sleep;
   I wake again, for the LORD sustains me.
I am not afraid of ten thousands of people
   who have set themselves against me round about.
—*Psalm 3:1-6 (RSV)*

O LORD, our Lord,
   how majestic is your name in all the earth!
You have set your glory
   above the heavens.
From the lips of children and infants
   you have ordained praise
   because of your enemies,
   to silence the foe and the avenger.
When I consider your heavens,
   the work of your fingers,

the moon and the stars,
   which you have set in place,
   what is man that you are mindful of him,
   the son of man that you care for him?
You made him a little lower than the
   heavenly beings
   and crowned him with glory and honor.
You made him ruler over the works of your hands;
   you put everything under his feet:
   all flocks and herds,
   and the beasts of the field,
   the birds of the air,
   and the fish of the sea,
   all that swim the paths of the seas.
O LORD, our Lord,
   how majestic is your name in all the earth!
—*Psalm 8*

Have mercy on me, O God,
   according to your unfailing love;
   according to your great compassion
   blot out my transgressions.
Wash away all my iniquity
   and cleanse me from my sin.
For I know my transgressions,
   and my sin is always before me.
Against you, you only, have I sinned
   and done what is evil in your sight,
   so that you are proved right when you speak
   and justified when you judge. . . .

Cleanse me with hyssop, and I will be clean;
  wash me, and I will be whiter than snow.
Let me hear joy and gladness;
  let the bones you have crushed rejoice.
Hide your face from my sins
  and blot out all my iniquity.
Create in me a pure heart, O God,
  and renew a steadfast spirit within me.
Do not cast me from your presence
  or take your Holy Spirit from me.
Restore to me the joy of your salvation
and grant me a willing spirit, to sustain me.
  . . . You do not delight in sacrifice,
  or I would bring it;
  you do not take pleasure in burnt offerings.
The sacrifices of God are a broken spirit;
  a broken and contrite heart,
  O God, you will not despise.
—*Psalm 51:1-4, 7-12, 16-17*

Hear my cry, O God;
  listen to my prayer.
From the ends of the earth I call to you,
  I call as my heart grows faint;
  lead me to the rock that is higher than I.
  For you have been my refuge,
  a strong tower against the foe.
I long to dwell in your tent forever
  and take refuge in the shelter of your wings.

For you have heard my vows, O God;
   you have given me the heritage of
   those who fear your name.
—Psalm 61:1-5

O God, you are my God,
   earnestly I seek you;
   my soul thirsts for you,
   my body longs for you,
   in a dry and weary land
   where there is no water.
I have seen you in the sanctuary
   and beheld your power and your glory.
Because your love is better than life,
   my lips will glorify you.
I will praise you as long as I live,
   and in your name I will lift up my hands.
My soul will be satisfied
   as with the richest of foods;
   with singing lips my mouth will praise you.
On my bed I remember you;
   I think of you through the watches of the night.
Because you are my help,
   I sing in the shadow of your wings.
My soul clings to you;
   your right hand upholds me.
—Psalm 63:1-8

Rescue me, O God! Lord, hurry to my aid! They are
after my life, and delight in hurting me. Confuse
them! Shame them! Stop them! Don't let them keep
on mocking me! But fill the followers of God with
joy. Let those who love your salvation exclaim,
"What a wonderful God he is!" But I am in deep
trouble. Rush to my aid, for only you can help and
save me. O Lord, don't delay.
—*Psalm 70* (TLB)

How lovely is your dwelling place,
O LORD Almighty!
My soul yearns, even faints,
for the courts of the LORD;
my heart and my flesh cry out
for the living God. . . .
Blessed are those who dwell in your house;
they are ever praising you.
Blessed are those whose strength is in you,
who have set their hearts on pilgrimage. . . .
Better is one day in your courts
than a thousand elsewhere;
I would rather be a doorkeeper in
the house of my God
than dwell in the tents of the wicked.
For the LORD God is a sun and shield;
the LORD bestows favor and honor;
no good thing does he withhold
from those whose walk is blameless.
O LORD Almighty,

blessed is the man who trusts in you.
—*Psalm 84:1-2, 4-5, 10-12*

LORD, you have been our dwelling place
throughout all generations.
Before the mountains were born
    or you brought forth the earth and the world,
    from everlasting to everlasting you are God.
. . . For a thousand years in your sight
    are like a day that has just gone by,
    or like a watch in the night.
You sweep men away in the sleep of death;
    they are like the new grass of the morning—
    though in the morning it springs up new,
    by evening it is dry and withered. . . .
Who knows the power of your anger?
For your wrath is as great as the fear that
    is due you.
Teach us to number our days aright,
    that we may gain a heart of wisdom.
Relent, O LORD! How long will it be?
Have compassion on your servants.
Satisfy us in the morning with your unfailing love,
    that we may sing for joy and
    be glad all our days.
Make us glad for as many days as
    you have afflicted us,
    for as many years as we have seen trouble.
May your deeds be shown to your servants,
    your splendor to their children.

May the favor of the Lord our God
   rest upon us;
   establish the work of our hands for us—
   yes, establish the work of our hands.
   —*Psalm 90:1-2,4-6,11-17*

My heart is steadfast, O God, my heart is steadfast;
   I will sing and make melody.
Awake, my soul!
Awake, O harp and lyre!
I will awaken the dawn.
I will give thanks to you, O LORD, among the
   peoples;
   and I will sing praises to you among the nations.
For your steadfast love is higher than the heavens,
   and your faithfulness reaches to the clouds.
Be exalted, O God, above the heavens,
   and let your glory be over all the earth.
   —*Psalm 108:1-5 (NRSV)*

O LORD, you have searched me and you know me.
You know when I sit and when I rise;
   you perceive my thoughts from afar.
You discern my going out and my lying down;
   you are familiar with all my ways.
Before a word is on my tongue
   you know it completely, O LORD.
. . . Where can I go from your Spirit?
Where can I flee from your presence?

If I go up to the heavens, you are there;
  if I make my bed in the depths, you are there.
If I rise on the wings of the dawn,
  if I settle on the far side of the sea,
  even there your hand will guide me,
  your right hand will hold me fast.
If I say, "Surely the darkness will hide me
  and the light become night around me,"
  even the darkness will not be dark to you;
  the night will shine like the day,
  for darkness is as light to you.
For you created my inmost being;
  you knit me together in my mother's womb.
I praise you because I am fearfully and
  wonderfully made;
  your works are wonderful,
  I know that full well.
My frame was not hidden from you
  when I was made in the secret place.
When I was woven together in the depths of
  the earth,
  your eyes saw my unformed body.
All the days ordained for me
  were written in your book
  before one of them came to be.
. . . Search me, O God, and know my heart;
  test me and know my anxious thoughts.
See if there is any offensive way in me,
  and lead me in the way everlasting.
—*Psalm 139:1-4, 7-16, 23-24*

Prayers of New Testament Believers

Following is the only prayer recorded in the Bible prayed by the New Testament church. It occurs after Peter and John's release from the authorities—they have all now been warned not to speak about Jesus in public.

Sovereign Lord, you made the heaven and the earth and the sea, and everything in them. You spoke by the Holy Spirit through the mouth of your servant, our father David:

"Why do the nations rage
  and the peoples plot in vain?
The kings of the earth take their stand
  and the rulers gather together against the Lord
  and against his Anointed One."

Indeed Herod and Pontius Pilate met together with the Gentiles and the people of Israel in this city to conspire against your holy servant Jesus, whom you anointed. They did what your power and will had decided beforehand should happen. Now, Lord, consider their threats and enable your servants to speak your word with great boldness. Stretch out your hand to heal and perform

miraculous signs and wonders through the name
of your holy servant Jesus.
—*Acts 4:24-30*

---

*In the New Testament church, believers waited eagerly for letters
from their spiritual leaders; often months would pass between
communications. These letters contained encouragement, instruction, doctrine, and occasionally words of discipline and
rebuke.*

*Prayers were also an intrinsic part of pastoral letters, especial-
ly those that survived of the apostle Paul. He wanted his
spiritual children to know what he said to God on their behalf.
These intercessions offer strength and insight and are still in-
voked by today's prayer warriors.*

Grace and peace to you from God our Father and
the Lord Jesus Christ.
—*1 Corinthians 1:3*

Praise be to the God and Father of our Lord Jesus
Christ, the Father of compassion and the God of all
comfort, who comforts us in all our troubles, so
that we can comfort those in any trouble with the
comfort we ourselves have received from God. For
just as the sufferings of Christ flow over into our
lives, so also through Christ our comfort overflows.
—*2 Corinthians 1:3-5*

Praise be to the God and Father of our Lord Jesus
Christ, who has blessed us in the heavenly realms
with every spiritual blessing in Christ. For he chose

us in him before the creation of the world to be
holy and blameless in his sight.
—*Ephesians 1:3-4*

I pray for you constantly, asking God, the glorious
Father of our Lord Jesus Christ, to give you wisdom to see clearly and really understand who
Christ is and all that he has done for you. I pray
that your hearts will be flooded with light so that
you can see something of the future he has called
you to share. I want you to realize that God has
been made rich because we who are Christ's have
been given to him! I pray that you will begin to understand how incredibly great his power is to help
those who believe him.
—*Ephesians 1:17-19 (TLB)*

I kneel before the Father, from whom his whole family in heaven and on earth derives its name. I pray
that out of his glorious riches he may strengthen you
with power through his Spirit in your inner being, so
that Christ may dwell in your hearts through faith.
And I pray that you, being rooted and established in
love, may have power, together with all the saints, to
grasp how wide and long and high and deep is the
love of Christ, and to know this love that surpasses
knowledge—that you may be filled to the measure of
all the fullness of God.
—*Ephesians 3:14-19*

Now unto him that is able to do exceeding abundantly above all that we ask or think, according to the power that worketh in us, Unto him be glory in the church by Christ Jesus throughout all ages, world without end. Amen.
—*Ephesians 3:20-21 (KJV)*

I thank my God every time I remember you. In all my prayers for all of you, I always pray with joy because of your partnership in the gospel from the first day until now, being confident of this, that he who began a good work in you will carry it on to completion until the day of Christ Jesus.
—*Philippians 1:3-6*

This is my prayer: that your love may abound more and more in knowledge and depth of insight, so that you may be able to discern what is best and may be pure and blameless until the day of Christ, filled with the fruit of righteousness that comes through Jesus Christ—to the glory and praise of God.
—*Philippians 1:9-11*

We always thank God, the Father of our Lord Jesus Christ, when we pray for you, because we have heard of your faith in Christ Jesus and of the love you have for all the saints—the faith and love that spring from the hope that is stored up for you in

heaven . . . For this reason, since the day we heard about you, we have not stopped praying for you and asking God to fill you with the knowledge of his will through all spiritual wisdom and understanding. And we pray this in order that you may live a life worthy of the Lord and may please him in every way: bearing fruit in every good work, growing in the knowledge of God, being strengthened with all power according to his glorious might so that you may have great endurance and patience, and joyfully giving thanks to the Father, who has qualified you to share in the inheritance of the saints in the kingdom of light. For he has rescued us from the dominion of darkness and brought us into the kingdom of the Son he loves, in whom we have redemption, the forgiveness of sins.
—Colossians 1:3-5, 9-14

How can we thank God enough for you in return for all the joy that we feel before our God because of you? Night and day we pray most earnestly that we may see you face to face and restore whatever is lacking in your faith.

Now may our God and Father himself and our Lord Jesus direct our way to you. And may the Lord make you increase and abound in love for one another and for all, just as we abound in love for you. And may he so strengthen your hearts in holiness that you may be blameless before our God

and Father at the coming of our Lord Jesus with all
his saints.
—*1 Thessalonians 3:9-13 (NRSVB)*

May our Lord Jesus Christ himself and God our
Father, who loved us and by his grace gave us eternal encouragement and good hope, encourage
your hearts and strengthen you in every good deed
and word.
—*2 Thessalonians 2:16-17*

I am grateful to God—whom I worship with a clear
conscience, as my ancestors did—when I remember
you constantly in my prayers night and day. Recall-
ing your tears, I long to see you so that I may be
filled with joy.
—*2 Timothy 1:3-4 (NRSVB)*

I always thank my God as I remember you in my
prayers, because I hear about your faith in the Lord
Jesus and your love for all the saints. I pray that
you may be active in sharing your faith, so that you
will have a full understanding of every good thing
we have in Christ.
—*Philemon 4-6*

---

*How does one say good-bye to fellow believers? What is the ap-
propriate end to a letter from prison or some faraway mission*

field? Following are the doxologies and benedictions written by the leaders of God's people through tumultuous political times as well as the formative years of the church as we know it.

May the grace of the Lord Jesus Christ, and the love of God, and the fellowship of the Holy Spirit be with you all.
—2 Corinthians 13:14

The grace of our Lord Jesus Christ be with your spirit, brethren. Amen.
—Galatians 6:18 (RSV)

Peace to the brothers, and love with faith from God the Father and the Lord Jesus Christ. Grace to all who love our Lord Jesus Christ with an undying love.
—Ephesians 6:23-24

To our God and Father be glory for ever and ever. . . . The grace of the Lord Jesus Christ be with your spirit. Amen.
—Philippians 4:20, 23

Grace be with you.
—Colossians 4:18

The very God of peace sanctify you wholly; and I
pray God your whole spirit and soul and body be
preserved blameless unto the coming of our Lord
Jesus Christ.
—*1 Thessalonians 5:23 (KJV)*

Now may the Lord of peace himself give you peace
at all times and in every way. The Lord be with all
of you.
—*2 Thessalonians 3:16*

The Lord be with your spirit. Grace be with you.
—*2 Timothy 4:22*

May the God of peace, who through the blood of
the eternal covenant brought back from the dead
our Lord Jesus, that great Shepherd of the sheep,
equip you with everything good for doing his will,
and may he work in us what is pleasing to him,
through Jesus Christ, to whom be glory for ever
and ever. Amen.
—*Hebrews 13:20-21*

And after you have suffered for a little while, the
God of all grace, who has called you to his eternal
glory in Christ, will himself restore, support,

strengthen, and establish you. To him be the power
forever and ever. Amen.
—*1 Peter 5:10-11* (NRSVB)

To him who is able to keep you from falling and to
present you before his glorious presence without
fault and with great joy—to the only God our
Savior be glory, majesty, power and authority,
through Jesus Christ our Lord before all ages, now
and forevermore! Amen.
—*Jude 24-25*

PRAYERS

OF THE

EARLY AND

MEDIEVAL

CHURCH

Introduction

What would a prayer of one of the first Christians sound
like? What words were recited in worship services of the
Apostles, of first-century Christians, of the parade of con-
gregations spanning the alternately dark and victorious
centuries prior to the Reformation? The nature of the early
church was such that relatively few personal devotions
remain in written form. Much of the time it was a persecuted church. Many of its members were illiterate. And
the lengthy creeds and histories now at our disposal were
as yet in formation.

Devotional materials attesting to the prayer lives of
early believers are available to us mainly in two forms:
writings of the monks, archbishops, scholars, and others in
the minority of educated believers; and the actual church
services that were printed in prayerbooks. Thus, many of
the following prayers are attributed to "Roman Breviary,"
"Liturgy of St. Mark," "Leonine Sacramentary," and so
forth. Sacramentaries, Liturgies, Breviaries, and such were
written materials used by the church in particular areas
and periods. Some are named for the bishop of that time;
others bear the name of their province or city. Few of the
dates or even origins are certain, however, so frequent was
the intermingling of worship forms as the various Christian communities came in contact with one another.

The prayers compiled in this section come from people
in an expansive cross section of geographical areas and
situations. Some of these believers are obviously going
through great stress and persecution. Prayers of others are
penned in the quiet study of an Augustine or Chrysostom
or some other monk, apologist, teacher, or Christian orator.

Their prayers, however, are surprisingly up-to-date.
They ask for the same graces, praise the same God, and
confess the same sins that we do in the twentieth century.
It is a special providence of God that the words of these

believers have survived wars, religious change, the weather, and—at times—general neglect. These timeless prayers refresh us today as we walk, struggle, and rejoice in the same Way, while the first people who uttered them watch from heaven, waiting for us and cheering us on.

Almighty Lord our God, direct our steps into the
way of peace, and strengthen our hearts to obey
your commands; may the Day-spring visit us from
on high, and give light to those who sit in darkness
and the shadow of death; that they may adore you
for your mercy, follow you for your truth, desire
you for your sweetness, who are the blessed Lord
God of Israel. Amen.
—*Ancient collect, undated*

Teach us, Holy Father . . .
to hope in your name, from whom everything
that exists has come.
Open our inward eyes
to recognize you, although you are
the highest in high heaven, and the holy one
among all the ranks of the holy.
You, Lord God,
bring down the proud and outwit the cunning;
promote the humble, and make the arrogant fall;
hold in your hand every issue of life—
whether we are to be rich or poor, whether
we are to live or die;
see every spirit, good or evil,
and the inner thoughts and intentions
of every person.
If we are in danger, you come to our aid.
If we are feeling desperate, you save us from
our own sense of failure.
If events in the world overshadow us, we remember

that you are the creator and overseer
of every living being.
—*St. Clement of Rome, 1st century, adapted*

Prayers of St. Polycarp, 1st-2nd centuries

◆   May God the Father, and the eternal high priest Jesus
Christ, build us up in faith and truth and love, and
grant to us our portion among the saints with all
those who believe on our Lord Jesus Christ. We pray
for all saints, for kings and rulers, for the enemies of
the cross of Christ, and for ourselves we pray that
our fruit may abound and we may be made perfect
in Christ Jesus our Lord. Amen.

◆   Lord God almighty, Father of your dear and
blessed Son Jesus Christ, through whom we have
been granted to know you; you are God over all;
over angels and other spiritual powers, over the
whole created universe, and over those good
people from every age who live in your presence.

I thank you today for the privilege of being
counted among those who have witnessed to you
with their lives; of sharing the cup of suffering
which Christ drank; and of rising again to life everlasting with him, in body and soul, and in the im-
mortality of the Holy Spirit.

May I be received today into your presence, a cost-
ly sacrifice and so an acceptable one. This is all part

of your plan and purpose, and you are now bringing it to pass. For you are the God of truth, and in
you is no falsehood at all.

For this, and for all the other things you have done
for me, I bless and glorify you, through our eternal
high priest in heaven, your dear Son, Jesus Christ,
who shares with you and the Holy Spirit glory for
ever. Amen.

As this piece of bread was scattered over the hills
and then was brought together and made one, so
let your church be brought together from the
ends of the earth into your kingdom. For yours is
the glory and the power through Jesus Christ
forever.
—*from the* **Didache,** *1st or 2nd century*

O Lord our God, who has bidden the light to shine
out of darkness, who has again wakened us to
praise your goodness and ask for your grace; accept now, in your endless mercy, the sacrifice of our
worship and thanksgiving, and grant unto us all
such requests as may be wholesome for us. Make
us to be children of the light and of the day, and
heirs of your everlasting inheritance. Remember, O
Lord, according to the multitude of your mercies,
your whole church; all who join with us in prayer,
all our brothers and sisters by land or sea, or

wherever they may be in your vast kingdom who
stand in need of your grace and succor. Pour out
upon them the riches of your mercy, so that we,
redeemed in soul and body, and steadfast in faith,
may ever praise your wonderful and holy name;
through Jesus Christ our Lord.

—*Greek church liturgy, 2nd century*

Give perfection to beginners, O Father; give intelligence to the little ones; give aid to those who are
running their course. Give sorrow to the negligent;
give fervor of spirit to the lukewarm. Give to the
perfect a good consummation; for the sake of
Christ Jesus our Lord.

—*attributed to St. Irenaeus, 2nd century*

O God, the Father of our Savior Jesus Christ . . .
sanctify, O Lord, our souls and bodies and spirits,
search our consciences, and cast out of us every
evil thought, every base desire, all envy and pride,
all wrath and anger, and all that is contrary to your
holy will. And grant us, O Lord . . . with a pure
heart and contrite soul, to call upon you, our holy
God and Father who is in heaven.

—*Liturgy of St. James, 2nd-5th centuries*

Bless all your people, the flocks of your fold. Send
down into our hearts the peace of heaven, and

grant us also the peace of this life. Give life to the souls of all of us, and let no deadly sin prevail against us, or any of your people. Deliver all who are in trouble, for you are our God, who sets the captives free; who gives hope to the hopeless, and help to the helpless; who lifts up the fallen; and who is the haven of the shipwrecked. Give your pity, pardon, and refreshment to every Christian soul, whether in affliction or error. Preserve us, in our pilgrimage through this life, from hurt and danger, and grant that we may end our lives as Christians, well-pleasing to you, and free from sin, and that we may have our portion and lot with all your saints; for the sake of Jesus Christ our Lord and Savior.
—*Liturgy of St. Mark, 2nd-5th centuries*

O God the Father, Origin of divinity, good beyond all that is good, fair beyond all that is fair, in whom is calmness, peace, and concord; make up the dissensions which divide us from each other, and bring us back into a unity of love, which may bear some likeness to your divine nature. And as you are above all things, make us one by the unanimity of a good mind, that through the embrace of charity and the bonds of affection, we may be spiritually one, as well in ourselves as in each other; through that peace of yours that makes all things peaceful, and through the grace, mercy, and tenderness of your son, Jesus Christ.
—*Dionysius the Great, 3rd century*

Keep us, O Lord, from the vain strife of words, and
grant to us a constant profession of the truth.
Preserve us in the faith, true and undefiled; so that
we may ever hold fast that which we professed
when we were baptized into the name of the
Father, and of the Son, and of the Holy Ghost; that
we may have you for our Father, that we may abide
in your Son, and in the fellowship of the Holy
Ghost; through the same Jesus Christ our Lord.
—*St. Hilary (of Poitiers), 4th century*

Lord Jesus, think on me and purge away my sin;
From earth-born passions set me free and make me
  pure within.

Lord Jesus, think on me, with care and woe
  oppressed;
Let me thy loving servant be and gain thy
  promised rest.

Lord Jesus, think on me nor let me go astray;
Through darkness and perplexity point thou the
  heavenly way.

Lord Jesus, think on me, that when the flood is past,
I may the eternal brightness see and share thy joy
  at last.
—*Synesius of Cyrene, 4th century*

O God of the ever-present crosses, help us, your servants.
—*Egypt, 4th century*

You have quieted those which were in confusion. Praise to your calmness! O Lord make quiet in your churches; and blend and unite, O Lord, the contentious sects; and still, and rule also the conflicting parties, and may there be at every time one true church, and may her righteous children gather themselves together to confess your graciousness. Praise to your reconciliation, O Lord God.
—*St. Ephraem the Syrian, 4th century*

Prayers of St. Chrysostom, 4th century

♦ We will sing unto the Lord a new song. O Lord you are great and glorious, wonderful in strength and invincible. Let all creatures serve you, for you spoke and they were made. You sent forth your spirit and they were created. O God, you are worthy to be praised with all pure and holy praise, therefore let your saints praise you with all thy creatures, and let all your angels and your elect praise you forever. Let our soul bless God, the great King, for worthy is the Lamb that was slain to receive power and riches, and wisdom, and strength, and honor, and glory, and blessing, both now and evermore.

◆   Fulfil now, O Lord, the desires and petitions of
     your servants as may be most expedient for them,
     granting us in this world knowledge of your truth,
     and in the world to come life everlasting.

O Lord, our God, teach us, we beg of you, to ask
you in the right way for the right blessings. Steer
the vessel of our life towards yourself, tranquil
haven of all storm-tossed souls. Show us the
course in which we should go. Renew a willing
spirit within us. Let your Spirit curb our
wayward senses, and guide and enable us unto
that which is our true good, to keep your laws,
and in all our works evermore to rejoice in your
glorious and gladdening presence. For yours is
the glory and praise from all your saints, for ever
and ever.
—*St. Basil, 4th century, adapted*

O our God, who opens your hand, and fills all
things living with plenteousness, unto you we commit all those who are dear to us; watch over them,
we beg of you, and provide all things needful for
their souls and bodies, from this time forth for evermore; through Jesus Christ our Lord.
—*St. Nerses, 4th century*

I have eaten at the head of the table, and now I wish to die at the head of my brothers, and mix my blood with theirs. With them I wish to come to know the life that holds neither suffering nor pain, that knows not the tyranny of victims. In that life I shan't be flayed by the threats of kings or the terrors of prefectures. Nor will anyone be able to drag me before the tribunal or make me tremble out of fear. In you shall I correct the errors of my past, O life of truth, in you my weary limbs will find repose, O Christ, sacred oil of our unction. In you all my sad soul-hurts vanish, for you are truly the cup of my salvation. You shall dry these tears from my eyes, O consolation and joy!

. . . The cross of our Lord protect those who belong to Jesus and strengthen your hearts in faith to Christ in hardship and in ease, in life and in death, now and forever.

—*Simeon Bar Sabbae, a bishop in Persia, martyred 4th century*

Prayers of St. Ambrose, 4th century

♦ Grant perfect rest to your servant, such rest as you have prepared for your saints. . . . May his soul pass to the region where he may no more feel the sting of death, and may he know that death is the end, not of being, but of Sin! . . . He returns now greater, and more glorious, more illustrious than an

earthly conqueror, surrounded not by his soldiers, but by the angelic hosts; not to his imperial city here, but to the heavenly city above.
—*prayer/oration at the funeral of the Roman emperor, Theodosius, 4th century*

♦ We pray you, O Creator of everything, at this hour preceding night, that you be clement and watch over us. Let dreams and phantoms of the night be scattered. Keep us safe from our enemies and make us pure!

♦ Jesu! look on us when we fall;
One momentary glance of yours
Can from her guilt the soul recall
To tears of penitence divine.

Awake us from false sleep profound,
And through our senses pour your light;
Be your blest name the first we sound
At early morn, the last at night.
—*from the hymn "At Cock-Crowing"*

Prayers of St. Augustine, 4th-5th centuries

♦ Grant us, even us, O Lord, to know you, and love you, and rejoice in you. And if we cannot do these perfectly in this life, let us, at least, advance to higher degrees every day, till we can come to do them in perfection. Let the knowledge of you increase in us here, that it may be full hereafter. Let the love of you grow every day more and more here, that it may be perfect hereafter; that our joy may be great in itself and full in you. We know, O God, that you are a God of truth. O make good your gracious promises to us, that our joy may be full. To your honor and glory, who with the Father and the Holy Ghost lives and reigns one God, world without end.

♦ Look upon us, O Lord, and let all the darkness of our souls vanish before the beams of your brightness. Fill us with holy love, and open to us the treasures of your wisdom. All our desire is known unto you, therefore perfect what you have begun, and what your Spirit has awakened us to ask in prayer. We seek your face; turn your face unto us and show us your glory, then shall our longing be satisfied, and our peace shall be perfect; through Jesus Christ our Lord.

♦ Watch, dear Lord, with those who wake, or watch, or weep to-night, and give your angels charge over those who sleep. Tend your sick ones, O Lord Christ. Rest your weary ones. Bless your dying ones. Soothe your suffering ones. Pity your afflicted ones. Shield your joyous ones. And all, for your love's sake. Amen.

♦ O Lord, help us to turn and seek you; for you have not forsaken your creatures as we have forsaken you, our Creator. Let us turn and seek you, for we

know you are here in our hearts, when we confess
to you, when we cast ourselves upon you, and
weep in your bosom, after all our rugged ways;
and you gently wipe away our tears, and we weep
the more for joy; because you, Lord, who made us,
do remake and comfort us.

Show your mercy to me, O Lord, to make my heart
glad. Let me find you, for whom I long. Lo, here
the man that was caught of thieves, wounded, and
left for half dead, as he was going towards Jericho.
You kind-hearted Samaritan, take me up. I am the
sheep that is gone astray; O good Shepherd, seek
me out, and bring me home to your fold again.
Deal favorably with me according to your good
pleasure, that I may dwell in your house all the
days of my life, and praise you for ever and ever
with them that are there.
—*St. Jerome, 4th-5th centuries*

Prayers of Egyptian believers, 4th-6th centuries

♦   Master Lord God almighty the Father of our Lord
and our God and our Saviour Jesus Christ, we give
thanks to you as touching all things and for all
things and in all things because you have sheltered
us, you have succored us, you have kept us, you
have redeemed us unto yourself, you have spared
us, you have helped us, you have brought us to this

hour. For this cause we pray and beseech your
goodness, O lover of man, grant us to accomplish
this holy day also and all the days of our life in all
peace and your fear. All envy, all temptation, all
working of Satan, the counsel of evil men, the upris-
ing of enemies secret and open, take away from us,
and from all your people, and from this holy place
of yours: but those things that are good and those
that are expedient supply unto us.
—*Coptic Jacobites*

♦   Lord almighty, Father of the Lord and our Saviour
Jesus Christ, we give you thanks for that you have
granted us to take of your holy mystery. Let it not
be unto guilt nor unto judgment but unto renewing
of soul and body and spirit: through your only Son
through whom to you with him and with the Holy
Ghost be glory and dominion eternally both now
and ever and world without end. Amen.
—*Ethiopic liturgy*

♦   The Lord give us, his servants, the blessing of
peace. Remission be unto us who have received
your body and your blood. Suffer us through the
Spirit to tread upon all the power of the enemy. The
blessing of your holy hand which is full of mercy,
even that we all hope for. From every evil work
turn us away, in every good work join us. Blessed
be he who has given us his holy body and his precious blood. We have taken of grace and we have

found life by the power of the cross of Jesus Christ.
Unto you, Lord, do we give thanks, after taking of
the grace that is from the Holy Ghost.
—*Abyssinian Jacobites*

May the strength of God pilot us. May the power of
God preserve us. May the wisdom of God instruct
us. May the hand of God protect us. May the way
of God direct us. May the shield of God defend us.
May the host of God guard us against the snares of
the evil one and the temptations of the world. May
Christ be with us. Christ before us. Christ in us,
Christ over us. May your salvation, O Lord, be al-
ways ours this day and for evermore. Amen.
—*St. Patrick, 5th century*

O God of love, who has given a new command-
ment through your only begotten Son, that we
should love one another, even as you did love us,
the unworthy and the wandering, and gave your
beloved Son for our life and salvation; we pray
you, Lord, give to us, your servants, in all time of
our life on the earth, a mind forgetful of past ill-
will, a pure conscience and sincere thoughts, and a
heart to love our brethren; for the sake of Jesus
Christ, your Son, our Lord and only Saviour.
—*Coptic liturgy of St. Cyril, 5th century*

O Heavenly Father, in whom we live and move
and have our being, we humbly pray you so to
guide and govern us by your Holy Spirit, that in all
the cares and occupations of our daily life we may
never forget you, but remember that we are ever
walking in your sight; for your own name's sake.
—*prayerbook, 5th century*

Yes, Lord, you are the God of all.
Yes, Lord, you are the King of all.
Yes, Lord, you are the Almighty.
Yes, Lord, you are the Governor of all.
Yes, Lord, you are the Savior of all.
Yes, Lord, you are the Judge of all.
Yes, Lord, you are the Life-giver of all.
Yes, Lord, you are the Keeper of all.
Yes, Lord, you are the Nourisher of all.
—*Patriarch of Antioch, 5th century*

Help us, O Lord, always to wait for you, to wish for
you, and to watch for you, that at your coming again
you may find us ready; for your sake we ask it.
—*prayerbook, 5th century*

We implore you, by the memory of your cross's hal-
lowed and most bitter anguish, make us fear you,
make us love you, O Christ.
—*St. Bridget, 5th-6th centuries*

Byzantine prayers (Armenian branch), early as 5th century

♦   We entreat and beseech with sighs and tears from all our souls your glorious creatorship, O incorruptible and uncreated timeless merciful Spirit, who is our advocate with the Father of mercies with groanings unutterable, who keeps the saints and cleanses sinners and makes them temples of the living and saving will of the most high Father: set us now free from all unclean deeds that are not conformable to your indwelling, that the light of your grace which enlightens the eyes of our mind be not quenched within us, for that we are taught that it is by prayer and the incense of a godly life that we are united with you.

♦   Holy Ghost who is the fountain of life and the spring of mercy, have mercy on this people which bowed down adores your godhead: keep them entire and stamp upon their hearts the posture of their bodies for the inheritance and possession of good things to come.

♦   Keep us in peace, O Christ our God, under the protection of your holy and venerable cross: save us from enemies visible and invisible and account us worthy to glorify you with thanksgiving with the Father and the Holy Ghost now and ever and world without end.

Prayers of Syrian believers (Jacobite branch), early as 5th century

♦ Grant us, O Lord God, the knowledge of your divine words and fill us with the understanding of your holy gospel and the riches of your divine gifts and the indwelling of your Holy Spirit and help us with joy to keep your commandments and accomplish them and fulfil your will and to be accounted worthy of the blessings and the mercies that are from you now and at all times.

♦ Our end preserve Christian and sinless and gather us beneath the feet of your elect when you will and where you will and as you will, only without shame by reason of our faults, that in this as in all things your all-honored and blessed name may be glorified and extolled with the name of our Lord Jesus Christ and your Holy Spirit now and ever and world without end.

Prayers of Persian believers (Nestorian branch), 6th century

♦ Pardon, O my Lord, by your compassion the sins and transgressions of your servants and hallow our lips by your grace that they may yield the fruits of praise to your exalted godhead with all your saints in your kingdom.

♦ When the sweet savor of the fragrance of your love is wafted upon us, O our Lord and our God, and

our souls are enlightened by the knowledge of your
truth, may we be accounted worthy to receive the
revelation of your beloved who is from heaven; and
there may we confess you and praise you without
ceasing in your crowned church which is full of all
helps and blessings; for you are lord and creator of
all, Father and Son and Holy Ghost, for ever.

Prayers of St. Gregory, 6th century

◆   O God, who for our redemption did give your only
     begotten Son to the death of the cross, and by his
     glorious resurrection has delivered us from the
     power of the enemy, grant us to die daily to sin,
     that we may evermore live with him, in the joy of
     his resurrection; through the same Jesus Christ our
     Lord.

◆   God, who as at this time did teach the hearts of
     your faithful people by sending to them the light of
     your Holy Spirit, grant us by the same Spirit to
     have a right judgment in all things, and evermore
     to rejoice in his holy comfort; through the merits of
     Christ Jesus our Savior, who lives and reigns with
     you in the unity of the same Spirit, one God, world
     without end.

Prayers from Mozarabic liturgies, 6th-8th centuries

◆   Be, O Lord, our protection, who is our redemption;
     direct our minds by your gracious presence, and

watch over our paths with guiding love; that, among the snares which lie hidden in this path in which we walk, we may so pass onward with hearts fixed on you, that by the track of faith we may come to be where you would have us.

♦ Hear us, O never-failing light, Lord our God, the fountain of light, the light of your angels, principalities, powers, and of all intelligent beings; who has created the light of your saints. May our souls be lamps of yours, kindled and illuminated by you. May they shine and burn with the truth, and never go out in darkness and ashes. May the gloom of sins be cleared away, and the light of perpetual faith abide within us.

♦ Jesus, our Master, do meet us while we walk in the way, and long to reach the Country; so that, following your light, we may keep the way of righteousness, and never wander away into the darkness of this world's night, while you, who are the way, the truth, and the life, are shining within us; for your own name's sake.

♦ O Heavenly Father, we bend the knee before you on behalf of all kings, princes, and governors of this world, asking you to give them, by your inspiration, the ability to rule in righteousness, to rejoice in peace, to shine in piety, and to labor for the well-being of the people committed unto them, so that, by the rectitude of the government, all faith-

ful people may live without disturbance in the knowledge of you, and the labor without hindrance for your glory; through Jesus Christ our Lord.
—*adapted*

Prayers from the Leonine Sacramentary, 7th century

◆ Almighty and everlasting God, who is always more ready to hear than we are to pray, and wants to give more than we either desire or deserve, pour down upon us the abundance of your mercy, forgiving us those things we are afraid of, and giving us those good things for which we are not worthy to ask, but through the merits and mediation of Jesus Christ, your Son, our Lord.
—*adapted*

◆ Grant us, O Lord, not to mind earthly things, but to love things heavenly; and even now, while we are placed among things that are passing away, to cleave to those that shall abide; through Jesus Christ our Lord.

◆ We beseech you, O Lord, be gracious to our times; that both national quietness and Christian devotion may be duly maintained by your bounty; through Jesus Christ our Lord. Amen.

◆ Be present, O Lord, to our prayers, and protect us by day as well as by night, that in all successive changes of time we may ever be strengthened by your unchangeableness; through Jesus Christ our Lord.

◆ O God, who in your loving-kindness does both begin and finish all good things; grant that as we glory in the beginnings of your grace, so we may rejoice in its completion; through Jesus Christ our Lord.

Prayers from the Gelasian Sacramentary, 8th century

◆ O God, forasmuch as our strength is in you, mercifully grant that your Holy Spirit may in all things direct and rule our hearts, through Jesus Christ our Lord.

◆ Almighty and everlasting God, who has revealed your glory by Christ among all nations, preserve the works of your mercy; that your church, which is spread throughout the world, may persevere with steadfast faith in confession of your name; through Jesus Christ our Lord.
—*intercessions for Good Friday*

◆ Into your hands, O God, we commend ourselves and all who are dear to us this day. Let the gift of your special presence be with us even to its close. Enable us never to lose sight of you all the day long, but to worship and pray to you, that at eventide we may again give thanks unto you; through Jesus Christ our Lord.

◆   Almighty and everlasting God, be present with us
      in all our duties, and grant the protection of your
      presence to all that dwell in this house, that you
      may be known to be the defender of this household
      and the inhabitant of this dwelling; through Jesus
      Christ our Lord.

O eternal Light, shine into our hearts. O eternal
Goodness, deliver us from evil. O eternal Power, be
our support. Eternal Wisdom, scatter the darkness
of our ignorance. Eternal Pity, have mercy upon us.
Grant unto us that with all our hearts, and minds,
and strength, we may evermore seek your face; and
finally bring us, in your infinite mercy, to your holy
presence. So strengthen our weakness that, following in the footsteps of your blessed Son, we may obtain your mercy, and enter into your promised joy.
—Alcuin, 8th century

Lord Jesus Christ, you did choose your apostles
that they might preside over us as teachers; so also
may it please you to teach doctrine to our bishops
in the place of your apostles, and to bless and instruct them, that they may preserve their lives un-
harmed and undefiled for ever and ever.
—Archbishop Egbert, 8th century

Lord God Almighty, shaper and ruler of all creatures, we pray for your great mercy, that you guide
us better than we have done, towards you. And
guide us to your will, to the need of our soul, better
than we can ourselves. And steadfast our mind
towards your will and to our soul's need. And
strengthen us against the temptations of the devil,
and put far from us all lust, and every unrighteous-
ness, and shield us against our foes, seen and unseen. And teach us to do your will, that we may
inwardly love you before all things, with a pure
mind. For you are our maker and our redeemer,
our help, our comfort, our trust, our hope; praise
and glory be to you now, ever and ever, world
without end.
—*Alfred the Great, 9th century*

The cross is the hope of Christians
the cross is the resurrection of the dead
the cross is the way of the lost
the cross is the savior of the lost
the cross is the staff of the lame
the cross is the guide of the blind
the cross is the strength of the weak
the cross is the doctor of the sick
the cross is the aim of the priests
the cross is the hope of the hopeless
the cross is the freedom of the slaves
the cross is the power of the kings

the cross is the water of the seeds
the cross is the consolation of the bondmen
the cross is the source of those who seek water
the cross is the cloth of the naked.
We thank you, Father, for the cross.
—*African hymn, 10th century*

Prayers of Leofric, Bishop of Exeter, 11th century

◆   Lord, we ask you to keep your household the
     church in continual godliness; that through your
     protection it may be free from all adversities, and
     devoutly given to serve you in good works, to the
     glory of your name; through Jesus Christ our Lord.

◆   Almighty God, unto whom all hearts be open, all
     desires known, and from whom no secrets are hid;
     cleanse the thoughts of our hearts by the inspira-
     tion of your Holy Spirit, that we may perfectly love
     you, and worthily magnify your holy name,
     through Christ our Lord. Amen.

Prayers from the Sarum Breviary, early as 11th century

◆   O God, who tells the number of the stars, and calls
     them all by their names; heal, we beg of you, the
     contrite in heart, and gather together the outcasts,
     and enrich us with the fullness of your wisdom;
     through Christ our Lord.

♦ Pour upon us, O Lord, the spirit of brotherly kindness and peace; so that, sprinkled with the dew of your benediction, we may be made glad by your glory and grace; through Christ our Lord.

♦ O God, of surpassing goodness, whom the round world with one voice does praise for your sweet kindness; we pray you to remove from us all error, that so we may perform your will; through Jesus Christ our Lord.

♦ O God, the renewer and lover of innocency, turn the hearts of all your servants to yourself, that they may be found ever rooted in faith and fruitful in works; through Jesus Christ our Lord.

Prayers of St. Anselm, 11th century

♦ O Lord our God, grant us grace to desire you with our whole heart; that so desiring we may seek and find you; and so finding you may love you; and loving you, may hate those sins from which you have redeemed us.

♦ O Lord my God,
my creator and my re-creator,
my soul longs for you.
Tell me what you are,
beyond what I have seen,
so that I may see clearly what I desire.

♦   We bring before you, O Lord, the troubles and
        perils of people and nations, the sighing of
        prisoners and captives, the sorrows of the
        bereaved, the necessities of strangers, the helpless-
        ness of the weak, the despondency of the weary,
        the failing powers of the aged. O Lord, draw near
        to each; for the sake of Jesus Christ our Lord.

Prayers from the Roman Breviary, 11th century and earlier

♦   O God, who has given us your Son to be an ex-
        ample and a help to our weakness in following the
        path that leads to life, grant us so to be his disciples
        that we may tread in his footsteps; for his name's
        sake.

♦   Grant, we beg of you, almighty God, unto us who
        know that we are weak, and who trust in you be-
        cause we know that you are strong, the gladsome
        help of your lovingkindness, both here in time and
        hereafter in eternity.

♦   O almighty God, grant . . . that we whose trust is
        under the shadow of your wings, may, through the
        help of your power, overcome all evils that rise up
        against us; through Jesus Christ our Lord.

Prayers from St. Bernard of Clairvaux, 12th century

♦   What thou, my Lord, hast suffered was all for
        sinners' gain;

Mine, mine was the transgression, but thine the
    deadly pain.
Lo, here I fall, my Savior! Tis I deserve thy place;
Look on me with thy favor, vouchsafe to me thy
    grace.

What language shall I borrow to thank thee,
    dearest friend,
for this thy dying sorrow, thy pity without end?
O make me thine forever, and should I fainting be,
Lord, let me never, never outlive my love to thee.
—*attributed to St. Bernard of Clairvaux*

♦   Jesus thou joy of loving hearts,
    thou fount of life, thou light of men,
    from the best bliss that earth imparts,
    we turn unfilled to thee again.

Thy truth unchanged hath ever stood;
    thou savest those that on thee call;
    to them that seek thee, thou art good,
    to them that find thee, all in all.

We taste thee, O thou living Bread,
    and long to feast upon thee still;
    we drink of thee, the fountainhead,
    and thirst our souls from thee to fill.

Our restless spirits yearn for thee,
    where'er our changeful lot is cast;
    glad, when thy gracious smile we see,
    blest, when our faith can hold thee fast.

O Jesus, ever with us stay,
make all our moments calm and bright;
chase the dark night of sin away,
shed o'er the world thy holy light.

Lord Jesus Christ, Son of the living God, who for
our redemption was born, and on the cross died
the most shameful of deaths, do by your death and
passion deliver us from all sins and penalties, and
by your holy Cross bring us, miserable sinners, to
that place where you live and reign with the Father
and the Holy Spirit, ever one God, world without
end.
—*Innocent III, 12th century*

Praised be my Lord, through those who forgive
from love of Thee,
And who suffer misery and hardship;
Happy are those who are patient in peace,
For they have received their crown from Thee,
    O Highest!

Praised be thou, my Lord, with thy creatures,
Especially our noble brother sun,
Who makes the day, and through him thou dost
    light us.
And it is fair and radiant with mighty splendour;

Of thee, O highest, a living image!

Praised be thou, my Lord, through our sisters,
    moon and stars!
In heaven thou hast formed them, so clear, and
    rich, and fair!
Praised be thou, my Lord, through our brother
    wind,
Through air and cloud and fair or evil weather,
For all thy creatures sustenance thou givest!

Praised be thou, my Lord, through our sister water,
Who is most useful, humble, rich and chaste!
Praised be thou, my Lord, through our brother fire,
Through which thou dost illuminate the night,
And it is fair and merry, sturdy, strong!

Praised be thou, my Lord, through our sister,
    mother earth,
Who us sustains and governs,
And beareth diverse fruits, with coloured flowers
    and grasses . . .
—*St. Francis of Assissi, 12th-13th centuries*

Thanks be to you, our Lord Jesus Christ,
for all the benefits that you have given us,
for all the pains and insults that you have borne
    for us.
Most merciful Redeemer, Friend, and Brother,

may we know you more clearly,
love you more dearly,
and follow you more nearly,
day by day.
—*St. Richard, 13th century*

Lord, you are my lover,
My longing,
My flowing stream,
My sun,
and I am your reflection.
—*St. Mechthild of Magdeburg, 13th century*

As the needle naturally turns to the north when it
is touched by the magnet, so it is fitting, O Lord,
that your servant should turn to love and praise
and serve you; seeing that out of love for him you
were willing to endure such grievous pangs and
sufferings.
—*Raymond Lull, 13th century*

Grant me, I beg of you, almighty and most merciful
God, fervently to desire, wisely to search out, and perfectly to fulfil, all that is well-pleasing to you. Order
my worldly condition to the glory of your name; and,
of all that you require me to do, grant me the
knowledge, the desire, and the ability, that I may so
fulfil it as I ought, and may my path to you, I pray, be

safe, straightforward, and perfect to the end.

Give me, O Lord, a steadfast heart, which no unworthy affection may drag downwards; give me an unconquered heart, which no tribulation can wear out; give me an upright heart, which no unworthy purpose may tempt aside.

Bestow upon me also, O Lord my God, understanding to know you, diligence to seek you, wisdom to find you, and a faithfulness that may finally embrace you. Amen.

—*St. Thomas Aquinas, 13th century*

O eternal Trinity
Eternal Trinity!
O fire and deep well of charity!
O you who are madly in love
with your creature!
O eternal truth!
O eternal fire!
O eternal wisdom!
Grant us your gentle and eternal benediction.
Amen.

—*St. Catherine (of Siena), 14th century*

Lord, I hereby surrender my will and my love; you have brought them to the point of surrender. I had thought that my calling was always to live in love through the promptings of my will. But now both love and will—which brought me out of my

spiritual childhood—are dead in me, and in this
death I find my freedom.
—*Marguerite Porete, 14th century*

God, of your goodness, give me yourself; for you are
sufficient for me. I cannot properly ask anything less,
to be worthy of you. If I were to ask less, I should always be in want. In you alone do I have all.
—*Julian of Norwich, 14th century*

God, unto whom all hearts be open, and unto whom
all will speaks, and unto whom no privy thing is hid.
I beseech you so for to cleanse the intent of my heart
with the unspeakable gift of your grace, that I may
perfectly love you, and worthily praise you.
—*from* **Cloud of Unknowing,** *14th century*

May Jesus Christ, the King of glory, help us to
make the right use of all the myrrh (i.e., suffering)
that God sends, and to offer to him the true incense
of our hearts; for his name's sake. Amen.
—*John Tauler, 14th century*

O Lord Jesus, acknowledge what is yours in us,
and take away from us all that is not yours; for
your honor and glory. Amen.
—*St. Bernardine, 14th-15th centuries*

Prayers of Thomas à Kempis, 14th-15th centuries

◆ Give us, O Lord, steadfast hearts that cannot be dragged down by false loves; give us courageous hearts that cannot be worn down by trouble; give us righteous hearts that cannot be sidetracked by unholy or unworthy goals. Give to us also, our Lord and God, understanding to know you, diligence to look for you, wisdom to recognize you, and a faithfulness that will bring us to see you face to face.

—*adapted*

◆ Ah Lord God, holy lover of my soul, when you come into my soul, all that is within me shall rejoice. You are my glory and the exultation of my heart; you are my hope and refuge in the day of my trouble. Set me free from all evil passions, and heal my heart of all inordinate affections; that, being inwardly cured and thoroughly cleansed, I may be made fit to love, courageous to suffer, steady to persevere. Nothing is sweeter than love, nothing more courageous, nothing fuller nor better in heaven and earth; because love is born of God, and cannot rest but in God, above all things. Let me love you more than myself, nor love myself but for your sake.

PRAYERS

OF THE

REFORMATION

AND

BEYOND

Introduction

Of all the prayers that have been uttered, just a few—a fraction—have been preserved in writing. As the church has experienced reformations, reawakenings, schism, births of new denominations and charitable orders, political oppression, expansion, and revival, the prayers of people in the midst of the changes have been captured, much as important moments in family life are captured by a few photographs.

We usually don't have pictures of the daily cooking and cleaning, but of birthdays, graduations, and Christmas. Except in the case of avid journal keepers, we have no record of the daily, mundane prayers of ordinary Christians. What we do have are prayers of writers and poets, of those embattled in controversy or reform, and of visionaries and leaders who perceived that what they said and prayed could set the pace or open the eyes of God's church at large.

So we can read what Martin Luther prayed, or the Archbishop of Canterbury, sister Teresa of Avila, hymnwriter Charles Wesley, missionary Jim Elliot, or political prisoner Dietrich Bonhoeffer. Their words become our family album—snapshots of a centuries-long history. It is ours for better understanding, meditation, and personal enrichment.

Good Lord, give us your grace, not to read or hear
this gospel of your bitter passion with our eyes and
our ears in manner of a pastime, but that it may
with compassion so sink into our hearts, that it
may stretch to the everlasting profit of our souls.
—*Sir Thomas More, 15th-16th centuries*

Prayers of Desiderius Erasmus, 15th-16th centuries

♦   O you who are the true Sun of the world, evermore
rising, and never going down; who, by your very
appearance nourishes and makes joyful all things—
those in heaven as well as those on earth—we ask
you to mercifully and favorably shine into our
hearts, that the night and darkness of sin, and the
mists of error on every side will be driven away, as
you shine brightly within our hearts. May we all
our life long go without any stumbling or offense,
and may we walk as in the daytime, being pure
and clean from the works of darkness, and abound-
ing in all good works that you have prepared for us
to walk in.
—*adapted*

♦   O Lord Jesus Christ, who are the Way, the Truth,
and the Life, we pray you not to let us stray from
you, who are the Way, nor to distrust you, who are
the Truth, nor to rest in any other thing than you,
who are the Life. Teach us by your Holy Spirit what
to believe, what to do, and wherein to take our rest.
For your own name's sake we ask it. Amen.

Prayers of Martin Luther, 15th-16th centuries

◆   O Lord, we are not worthy to have a glimpse of
heaven, and unable with our works to redeem ourselves from sin, death, the devil, and hell. For this
we rejoice, praise and thank you, O God, that
without price and out of pure grace you have
granted us this boundless blessing in your dear Son
through whom you take sin, death, and hell from
us, and give to us all that belongs to him.

◆   Ah, dearest Jesus, Holy Child,
Make thee a bed, soft, undefiled,
Within my heart, that it may be
A quiet chamber kept for thee.

◆   We give thanks unto you, heavenly Father, through
Jesus Christ, your dear Son, that you have this day
so graciously protected us, and we beg you to forgive us all our sins, and the wrong which we have
done, and by your great mercy defend us from all
the perils and dangers of this night. Into your
hands we commend our bodies and souls, and all
that is ours. Let your holy angel have charge con-
cerning us, that the wicked one have no power
over us.

Prayers of Miles Coverdale, 15th-16th centuries

◆   O Lord God almighty, we thank you with all our
hearts, that you have fed our souls with the body
and blood of your most dear Son. And we beg you

so to illuminate our minds with your Holy Spirit, that we may daily increase in strength of faith to you, in assuredness of hope in your promises, and fervency of love toward you and our neighbor, to the glory and praise of your holy name.

♦   Have mercy upon our impatience, O merciful Father, and print in our hearts the image of your Son. Grant us grace to follow his footsteps; expel out of us all fear of worldly accusations and false judgments. . . . Let your love increase and grow in us and whatever is in us that strives against or resists your holy will, let the same become extinct and die.

Almighty God, the fountain of all wisdom, who knows our necessities before we ask, and our ignorance in asking; we ask you to have compassion upon our infirmities; and those things, which for our unworthiness we dare not, and for our blindness we cannot ask, vouchsafe to give us; for the worthiness of your Son Jesus Christ our Lord.
—*Book of Common Prayer, 16th century*

Prayers of Philip Melancthon, 16th century

♦   Almighty and holy Spirit, the comforter, pure, living, true—illuminate, govern, sanctify me, and confirm my heart and mind in the faith, and in all genuine consolation; preserve and rule over me that, dwelling in the house of the Lord all the days of my life, to behold the beauty of the Lord, I may be and remain forever in the temple of the Lord, and praise him with a joyful spirit, and in union with all the heavenly church.

♦   Comfort, O merciful Father, by your Word and Holy Spirit, all who are afflicted or distressed, and so turn their hearts unto you, that they may serve you in truth, and bring forth fruit to your glory. Be, O Lord, their succor and defense; through Jesus Christ our Lord.

Take, O Lord, and receive my entire liberty, my memory, my understanding, and my whole will. All that I am, all that I have, you have given me and I will give it back again to you to be disposed of according to your good pleasure. Give me only your love and your grace; with you I am rich enough, nor do I ask for aught besides. Amen.
—*St. Ignatius of Loyola, 16th century*

Prayers of John Knox, 16th century

♦   Give unto the mouth of your people truth and wisdom which no man may resist. And although we have most justly deserved this plague and famine of your Word, yet, upon our true repentance, grant . . . that we may be released [of that famine]. And here we promise, before your divine majesty,

better to use your gifts than we have done, and
more straitly to order our lives, according to your
holy will and pleasure; and we will ever sing
praises to your most blessed name.

♦ The great bishop of our souls, Jesus our Lord, so
strengthen and assist your troubled hearts with the
mighty comfort of the Holy Spirit, that neither
earthly tyrants, nor worldly torments, may have
power to drive you from the hope and expectation
of that kingdom, which for the elect was prepared
from the beginning, by our heavenly Father, to
whom be all praise and honor, now and ever.

♦ O God of all power, who has called from death the
great pastor of the sheep, our Lord Jesus, comfort
and defend the flock which he has redeemed by
the blood of the eternal testament; increase the
number of true preachers; mitigate and lighten the
hearts of the ignorant; relieve the pains of those
who are afflicted, but especially of those that suffer
for the testimony of the truth, by the power of our
Lord Jesus Christ.

O blessed Lord and loving Father, unless you direct
us we cannot stand, but shall fall into many sins;
for no estate, no degree, no calling, office, function,
or trade of life can prosper or be rightly performed
without your continual aid, direction, and
providence. Therefore, Lord, guide us by your

Spirit, increase our faith, give us wisdom and able-
ness in all things to execute our calling as we
ought. Be present, good and gracious Father, with
us, and grant that all things that we take in hand
may begin in knowledge, proceed in fear of you,
and end in love, that our whole course of life may
be blessed by you; for the sake of Christ Jesus our
Lord.
—*J. Norden, 16th century*

Instruct our mouth, O good Lord, with a new song,
that our hearts being renewed, we may sing in the
company of your saints, and rejoice in you our
creator and redeemer. Let us possess such peace of
conscience, that may strengthen work in you, and
being armed with the two-edged sword of your
word and Holy Spirit, we may strive against all
things that oppose themselves to the glory of your
most holy name; and that through Jesus Christ your
dear Son, our only Lord and redeemer. So be it.
—*Scottish Psalter, 16th century*

What shall befall us hereafter we know not; but to
God, who cares for all people, who will one day
reveal the secrets of all hearts, we commit ourselves
wholly, with all who are near and dear to us. And
we ask the same most merciful and almighty God,
that for the time to come we may so bear the
reproach of Christ with unbroken courage, as ever

to remember that here we have no continuing city,
but may seek one to come, by the grace and mercy
of our Lord Jesus Christ; to whom with the Father,
and the Holy Ghost, be all honor and dominion,
world without end.
—*Matthew Parker, 16th century*

Prayers of John Calvin, 16th century

♦   May we fly to your mercy, prostrate ourselves
before you in silence, and acknowledge no other
hope but your pity and the intercession of your only
begotten Son. May we be reconciled to you, ab-
solved from our sins and governed throughout the
whole course of our lives by your Holy Spirit. Let
us at length enjoy the victory in every kind of contest, and arrive at that blessed rest which you have
prepared for us by our Lord Jesus Christ.

♦   Almighty God, since so many of the people who
have been gathered by you have fallen away, and
have by their ingratitude alienated themselves
from the hope of eternal salvation, grant that they
may be reunited with us, and hold with us the true
unity of faith, so that with one heart and one mouth
we may profess you as our God and Father. May we
learn to live under your name, acknowledge you as
our judge, and ascribe to you all power over us, until
we shall at length enjoy that eternal inheritance, into
the hope of which you have called us and daily invite
us, through Christ Jesus our Lord.

We know, O Lord, the weakness of ourselves, and how ready we are to fall from you. Allow not Satan, therefore, to show his power and malice upon us; for we are not able to withstand his assaults. Arm us, O Lord, always with your grace, and assist us with your Holy Spirit in all kinds of temptations; through Jesus Christ our Lord.
—*Edmund Grindal, 16th century*

Give us new hearts, and renew your Holy Spirit within, O Lord, that both the rulers of our land may faithfully minister justice, punish sin, defend and maintain the preaching of your Word, and that all ministers may diligently teach your dearly beloved flock, purchased by the blood and death of your own, and only dear Son our Lord, and that all people may obediently learn and follow your law, to the glory of your holy name; for Christ's sake, our only Lord and Savior.
—*James Pilkington, 16th century*

Govern all by your wisdom, O Lord, so that my soul may always be serving you as you desire, and not as I may choose. Do not punish me, I beg you, by granting that which I wish or ask, if it offends your love, which would always live in me. Let me die to myself, that so I may serve you; let me live to you, who . . . are true life.
—*St. Teresa (of Avila), 16th century*

Grant, O heavenly father, that we may so faithfully believe in you, and so fervently love one another, always living in awe of you and in the obedience of your holy law and blessed will, that we, being fruitful in all good works, may lead our lives according to your good pleasure in this transitory world and, after this frail and short life, obtain the true and immortal life, where you live and reign, world without end.

—*Thomas Becon, 16th century*

Nothing, O Lord, is more like your holy nature than the mind that is settled in quietness. You have called us into that quietness and peace, from out of the turmoils of this world—as it were, from out of storms into a haven. It is a peace the world cannot give, and that surpasses all human capacity. Grant now, O most merciful Father, that, through your overwhelming goodness, our minds may yield themselves in obedience to you without striving; and that they may quietly rise into your sovereign rest. May nothing disturb or disquiet us here. Rather, let us be calm and quiet in your peace.

—*A book of Christian prayers, 16th century, adapted*

O Lord, who has taught us that all our doings without charity are worth nothing, send your Holy Spirit and pour into our hearts that most excellent

gift of charity, the very bond of peace and of all virtues, without which whoever lives is counted dead before you. Grant this for your only son Jesus Christ's sake.
—*Book of Common Prayer, 16th century*

O heavenly Father, the author and fountain of all truth, the bottomless sea of all understanding, send, we pray, your Holy Spirit into our hearts, and lighten our understanding with the beams of your heavenly grace. We ask this, O merciful Father, for thy dear Son, our Savior Jesus Christ's sake.
—*Nicholas Ridley, 16th century*

O Lord God of hosts, fill, we beg of you, all those whom you have set as pastors over your sheep, with righteousness and true holiness, that by their faith and piety they may overcome the wicked one, and save the Lord's flock from the danger of his assaults; through Jesus Christ our Lord.
—*Gothic missal, 16th century or earlier*

Prayers of Johann Arndt, 16th-17th centuries

♦ Ah, Lord, unto whom all hearts are open, you can govern the vessel of our souls far better than we can. Arise, O Lord, and command the stormy wind and the troubled sea of our hearts to be still, and at peace in you, that we may look up to you undisturbed, and

abide in union with you, our Lord. Let us not be
carried hither and thither by wandering thoughts,
but, forgetting all else, let us see and hear you.

◆   O loving and tender Father in heaven, we confess
before you, in sorrow, how hard and unsympa-
thetic are our hearts; how often we have sinned
against our neighbours by want of compassion and
tenderness; how often we have felt no true pity for
their trials and sorrows, and have neglected to comfort, help, and visit them. O Father, forgive this our
sin, and lay it not to our charge. Give us grace ever
to alleviate the crosses and difficulties of those
around us, and never to add to them; teach us to be
consolers in sorrow, to take thought for the
stranger, the widow, and the orphan; let our charity
show itself not in words only, but in deed and
truth. Teach us to judge as you do, with for-
bearance, with much pity and indulgence; and help
us to avoid all unloving judgment of others.

To God the Father, God the Son, and God the Spirit,
we pour out humble and hearty supplications. We
ask that he—remembering the calamities of
humanity and the pilgrimage of our lives on
earth—would open to us new consolations out of
the fountain of his goodness, so that our miseries
can be alleviated. We humbly and earnestly ask
that things of earthly life would not infringe upon
divine things . . . that we would not become so

haughty with our intellect that we think we can understand divine mysteries. Rather, Lord, purge our
minds of foolish fancies, subject to your will; help
us to give to faith what is faith's, so that we may
continually attain to a deeper knowledge and love
of you. For you are the fountain of light, and you
dwell in the light that no person can even approach.
—*Francis Bacon, 16th-17th centuries, adapted*

We pray for the people, that they make not themselves over-wise; but be persuaded by reason, and
yield to the authority of their superiors.

We pray for the kingdoms of the world, their
stability and peace; for our own nation, kingdom,
and empire, that they may abide in prosperity and
happiness, and be delivered from all peril and dis-
aster.

For the King, O Lord, save him; O Lord, give him
prosperity, compass him with the shield of truth
and glory, speak good things unto him, in behalf of
your church and people.

Unto all men everywhere give your grace and
blessing; through Jesus Christ.
—*Lancelot Andrewes, 16th-17th centuries*

I thank you, my creator and Lord, that you have
given me these joys in your creation, this ecstacy
over the works of your hands. I have made known
the glory of your works to men as far as my finite

spirit was able to comprehend your infinity. If I have
said anything wholly unworthy of you, or have
aspired after my own glory, graciously forgive me.
—*Johann Kepler, 16th-17th centuries*

Prayers of John Donne, 16th-17th centuries

◆   O Lord,
       never allow us to think that we can stand by our-
       selves, and not need you.

◆   Eternal and most glorious God, allow me not so to
       undervalue myself as to give away my soul—*your*
       soul, your dear and precious soul—for nothing;
       and all the world is nothing, if the soul must be
       given for it. . . . You alone steer my boat through all
       its voyage, and give it special care when it comes to
       a narrow current, or to a dangerous fall of waters.
       You take care of and preserve my body . . . enlarge
       your providence towards me so far that no illness
       or agony may shake and benumb the soul.
       —*adapted*

Thou hast given so much to me,
Give one thing more—a grateful heart;
Not thankful when it pleaseth me,
As if Thy blessings had spare days,
But such a heart whose pulse may be
Thy praise.
—*George Herbert, 17th century*

O God, the father of lights, from whom comes down every good and perfect gift; mercifully accept our thanksgivings, and look upon our frailty and infirmity, and grant us such health of body as you know to be needful for us; that both in body and soul, we may evermore serve you with all our strength and might; through Jesus Christ our Lord.

—*John Cosin, 17th century*

Prayers of Benjamin Jenks, 17th century

♦ Oh, teach us to know you, our God, and enable us to do your will as we ought to do. Give us hearts to love you, to trust and delight in you, and to adhere and cleave in faithfulness unto you. That no temptations may draw us, nor any tribulations drive us from you; but that all your dispensations to us, and all your dealings with us, may be the messengers of your love to our souls, to bring us still nearer to your blessed self, and to make us still fitter for your heavenly kingdom.

♦ O Lord God, the one God, make your people one. Whatever be our differences, even in matters essential, may we ever realize that we are all one in Christ Jesus. Let not Satan break the blessed bond of union between believers, but may it be increasingly strengthened in our own experience, and in all your people everywhere; for the sake of Jesus Christ our Redeemer.

Give us, O Lord, a mind after your own heart, that we may delight to do your will . . . let your law be written on our hearts. Give us courage and resolution to do our duty, and a heart to be spent in your service, and in doing all the good that possibly we can the few remaining days of our pilgrimage here on earth.

—*John Tillotson, 17th century*

Almighty and most merciful Father . . . Grant that Jesus our Lord . . . may be formed in us, in all humility, meekness, patience, contentedness, and absolute surrender of our souls and bodies to your holy will and pleasure. Leave us not, nor forsake us, O Father, but conduct us safe through all changes of our condition here, in an unchangeable love to you, and in holy tranquility of mind in your love to us, till we come to dwell with you, and rejoice in you forever.

—*Simon Patrick, 17th century*

Prayers of Jeremy Taylor, 17th century

♦   We pray unto you, O great King of heaven and earth, for all Christian kings, princes, governors, and states. Crown them with justice and peace, and with the love of God, and the love of their people. Let holiness unto the Lord be on their foreheads, invest them with the armour of righteousness, and let the anointing from above make them sacred, wise, and holy; that, being servants of the King of kings, friends of religion, ministers of justice, patrons of the poor, they may at last inherit a portion in the kingdom of our Lord and Savior Jesus Christ.

♦ Bless our children with healthful bodies, with good understandings, with the graces and gifts of your Spirit, with sweet dispositions and holy habits; and sanctify them throughout in their bodies, souls, and spirits, and keep them unblamable to the coming of our Lord Jesus.

O blessed Savior, draw us; draw us by the cords of your love; draw us by the sense of your goodness . . . draw us by the unspotted purity and beauty of your example; draw us by the merit of your precious death and by the power of your Holy Spirit; draw us, good Lord, and we shall run after you; for your name's sake.
—*Isaac Barrow, 17th century*

Prayers of Thomas Ken, 17th century

♦ O our God, amidst the deplorable division of your church, O let us never widen its breaches, but give us universal charity to all who are called by your name. O deliver us from the sins and errors, from the schisms and heresies of the age. O give us grace daily to pray for the peace of your church, and earnestly to seek it and to do all we can to praise

and to love you; through Jesus Christ, our one
Savior and Redeemer.

◆   Praise God, from whom all blessings flow,
      Praise him all creatures here below,
      Praise him above, angelic host,
      Praise Father, Son, and Holy Ghost.

O Lord, let me not henceforth desire health or life,
except to spend them for you, with you, and in
you. You alone know what is good for me; do,
therefore, what seems best. Give to me, or take
from me; conform my will to yours; and grant that,
with humble and perfect submission, and in holy
confidence, I may receive the orders of your eternal
providence; and may equally adore all that comes
to me from you; through Jesus Christ our Lord.
—*Blaise Pascal, 17th century*

Bles't be thy name who did'st restore
to health my daughter dear
When death did seem ev'n to approach
And life was ended near.
Grant she remember what you've done
And celebrate thy praise
And let her conversations say
She loves you all her days.
—*Anne Bradstreet, 17th century*

Infinite and eternal Majesty! Author and fountain of being and blessedness! How little do we poor sinful creatures know of you or the way to serve and please you! We talk of religion and pretend unto it; but alas! how few are there that know and consider what it means! How easily do we mistake the affections of our nature and the issues of self-love for those divine graces which alone can render us acceptable in your sight! It may justly grieve me to consider that I should have wandered so long and contented myself so often with vain shadows and false images of piety and religion; yet I cannot but acknowledge and adore your goodness, who has been pleased in some measure to open my eyes and let me see what mighty improvements my nature is capable of . . . Let me never cease my endeavors till that new and divine nature prevail in my soul and Christ be formed within me.
—*Henry Scougal, 17th century*

O Lord, lift up the light of your countenance upon us; let your peace rule in our hearts . . . keep us from sin. Give us the rule over our own spirits, and keep us from speaking unadvisedly with our lips. May we live together in peace and holy love, and do command your blessing upon us, even life forevermore. Prepare us for all the events of the day, for we know not what a day may bring forth. Give us grace to deny ourselves; to take up our

cross daily, and to follow in the steps of our Lord
and master, Jesus Christ our Lord.
—*Matthew Henry, 17th century*

Prayers of Francois Mothe Fenelon, 17th-18th centuries

♦   Lord, take my heart,
     for I cannot give it to you.
     And when you have it, keep it,
     for I would not take it from you.
     And save me in spite of myself,
     for Christ's sake.
     Amen.

♦   We ask not, O Father, for health or life. We make an
     offering to you of all our days. You have counted
     them. We would know nothing more. All we ask is
     to die rather than live unfaithful to you; and, if it be
     your will that we depart, let us die in patience and
     love. Almighty God, who holds in your hand the
     keys of the grave to open and close it at your will,
     give us not life, if we shall love it too well. Living
     or dying we would be yours.

♦   O Lord! I know not what I should ask of you. You
     only know what I want; and you love me . . . better
     than I can love myself. O Lord! Give to me . . . what
     is proper . . . I dare not ask either crosses or com-
     forts. I only present myself before you. I open my
     heart to you. Behold my wants, which I myself am

ignorant of; but . . . do according to your mercy.
Smite, or heal! Depress me, or raise me up. I adore
all your purposes without knowing them. I am
silent, I offer myself in sacrifice. I abandon myself
to you. . . . Lord, teach me how to pray! Dwell in
me by your Holy Spirit.

Prayers of Thomas Wilson, 17th-18th centuries

♦   O heavenly Father, subdue in us whatever is contrary to your holy will. Grant that we may ever
study to know your will, that we may know how
to please you. Grant, O God, that we may never
run into those temptations which in our prayers
we desire to avoid. Lord, never permit our trials
to be above our strength; through Jesus Christ
our Lord.

♦   O God . . . remember me in the day of trouble; keep
me from all excess of fear, concern, and sadness.
Grant me a humble and resigned heart, that, with
perfect control I may ever acquiesce in all the
methods of your grace; that I may never frustrate
the designs of your mercy by unreasonable fears,
by sloth, or self-love.

O God, our help in ages past, our hope for years
   to come,
Our shelter from the stormy blast, and our eternal
   home!

Under the shadow of thy throne, still may we
   dwell secure;
Sufficient is Thine arm alone, and our defense
   is sure.
Before the hills in order stood, or earth received
   her frame,
From everlasting thou art God, to endless years
   the same.
A thousand ages in thy sight are like an
   evening gone;
Short as the watch that ends the night, before the
   rising sun.
O God, our help in ages past, our hope for years
   to come,
Be thou our guide while life shall last, and our
   eternal home!
   —*Isaac Watts, 17th-18th centuries*

Prayers of Susanna Wesley, 17th-18th centuries

◆   Save me from leading an imaginary life in the ideas
of others, and so to be eager and forward in show-
ing myself to the world. Forbid that I should retain,
improve and adorn this fictitious being, while
stupidly neglecting the truth. Help me not to contend with men's interests, prejudices, and passions,
that rarely admit of a calm dispute, when it can in-
nocently be avoided. May I be so far a lover of
myself as to prefer the peace and tranquility of my
own mind before that of others, and if, after doing
all that I can to make others happy, they yet remain

obstinately bent to follow those ways that lead to misery, I leave them to your mercy.

♦ Help me, Lord, to remember that religion is not to be confined to the church or closet, nor exercised only in prayer and meditation, but that everywhere I am in your presence. So may my every word and action have a moral content.

Almighty God, our heavenly Father, without whose help labor is useless, without whose light search is vain, invigorate my studies, and direct my inquiries, that I may, by due diligence and right discernment, establish myself and others in your holy faith. Take not, O Lord, your Holy Spirit from me; let not evil thoughts have dominion in my mind. Let me not linger in ignorance, but enlighten and support me, for the sake of Jesus Christ our Lord.
—*Samuel Johnson, 18th century*

Prayers of Henry Martyn, 18th century

♦ Now may the Spirit, who gave the Word, and called me, I trust, to be an interpreter of it, graciously and powerfully apply it to the hearts of sinners.

♦ O send your light and your truth, that we may live always near to you, our God. Let us feel your love, that we may be as it were already in heaven, that we may do all our work as the angels do theirs. Let us be ready for every work, be ready to go out or come in, to stay or to depart, just as you shall appoint. Lord, let us have no will of our own, or consider our true happiness as depending in the slightest degree on anything that can befall us outwardly, but as consisting altogether in conformity to your will; through Jesus Christ our Lord.

♦ Blessed be God. My friends are alarmed about the solitariness of my future life, and my tendency to melancholy; but, O my dearest Lord! you are with me, your rod and your staff they comfort me. I go on your errand—and I know that you are and will be with me. How easily can you support and refresh my heart!

O ever blessed fountain of life, I bless you that you have infused into me your own vital breath, so that I have become a living soul. . . . Draw on my soul, by the gentle influences of your gracious Spirit, every trace and every feature that your eye, O heavenly Father, may survey with pleasure, and that you may acknowledge as your own image. I ask and hope it through him of whose fulness we have all received.
—*Philip Doddridge, 18th century*

Prayers of Gerhard Tersteegen, 18th century

♦ O Lord, your hands have formed us, and you have sent us into this world, that we may walk in the

way that leads to heaven and you, and may find a
lasting rest in you who are the source and center of
our souls. Look in pity on us poor pilgrims in the
narrow way; let us not go astray, but reach at last
our true home where our Father dwells. Guide and
govern us from day to day, and bestow on us food
and strength for body and soul, that we may jour-
ney on in peace. Forgive us for having so often
wavered or looked back, and let us march straight
on in the way of your laws, and may our last step
be a safe and peaceful passage to the arms of your
love, and the blessed fellowship of the saints in
light. Hear us, O Lord, and glorify your name in us
that we may glorify you for ever and ever.

♦   All-sufficing Being,
    Which I choose for me,
    Ever do I treasure;
    Thou alone sufficest,
    Inward, pure, complete,
    All within my spirit.
    Satisfied and still,
    Who on Thee depends
    Shall desire no more.

♦   Strengthen our souls, animate our cold hearts with
    your warmth and tenderness, that we may no more
    live as in a dream, but walk before you as pilgrims in
    earnest to reach their home. And grant us all at last to
    meet with your holy saints before your throne, and
    there rejoice in your love for ever and ever.

Prayers of John Wesley, 18th century

◆   Forgive them all, O Lord . . . :
      our sins of omission and our sins of commission;
      the sins of our youth and the sins of our riper years;
      the sins of our souls and the sins of our bodies;
      our secret and our more open sins;
      our sins of ignorance and surprise, and our more
      deliberate and presumptuous sins;
      the sins we have done to please ourselves and the
      sins we have done to please others;
      the sins we know and remember, and the sins we
      have forgotten;
      the sins we have striven to hide from others and
      the sins by which we have made others offend;
      forgive them, O Lord, forgive them all for his sake
      who died for our sins and rose for our justification,
      and now stands at your right hand to make inter-
      cession for us,
      Jesus Christ our Lord.

◆   O Lord, let us not live to be useless; for Christ's
      sake. Amen.

◆   Take the full possession of my heart, raise there
      your throne, and command there as you do in
      heaven. Being created by you, let me live to you.
      Being created for you, let me ever act for your
      glory. Being redeemed by you, let me render unto
      you what is yours, and let my spirit ever cleave to
      you alone.

Return, O holy Dove, return, sweet messenger
of rest;
I hate the sins that made thee mourn, and drove
thee from my breast.
The dearest idol I have known, whatever that
idol be,
Help me to tear it from thy throne, and worship
only thee.
So shall my walk be close with God, calm and
serene my frame;
So purer light shall mark the road that leads me to
the Lamb.
—*William Cowper, 18th century*

O God, upon my bended knees, I pray you, to
remove the iron hand of persecution, which now
rests upon your little flock. Can it be consistent
with your holy attributes, that *these* should perish
through the malignity and wickedness of *your*
enemies? That be far from you, to do after this manner, to slay the righteous with the wicked . . . shall
not the Judge of all the earth do right?
—*Thomas Coke, 18th century*

Prayers of Charles Wesley, 18th century

♦   Come, thou long expected Jesus, born to set thy
people free;
From our fears and sins release us; let us find our
rest in thee.

Israel's strength and consolation, hope of all the
earth thou art;
Dear Desire of every nation, joy of every longing
heart.
Born thy people to deliver, born a child and yet
a king.
Born to reign in us forever, now thy gracious
kingdom bring,
By thine own eternal Spirit, rule in all our
hearts alone;
By thine all sufficient merit, raise us to thy glorious
throne.

◆   Love divine, all loves excelling,
Joy of heaven to earth come down,
Fix in us thy humble dwelling,
All thy faithful mercies crown.
Jesus, thou art all compassion,
Pure, unbounded love thou art;
Visit us with thy salvation,
Enter every trembling heart.

We must praise your goodness, that you have left
nothing undone to draw us to yourself. But one
thing we ask of you, our God, not to cease your
work in our improvement. Let us tend towards
you, no matter by what means, and be fruitful in
good works, for the sake of Jesus Christ our Lord.
—*Ludwig von Beethoven, 18th-19th centuries*

Lord I want to be a Christian in-a my heart, in-a
my heart,
Lord I want to be a Christian in-a my heart.
Lord I want to be more loving in-a my heart, in-a
my heart,
Lord I want to be more loving in-a my heart.
Lord I want to be more holy in-a my heart, in-a
my heart,
Lord I want to be more holy in-a my heart.
Lord I want to be like Jesus in-a my heart, in-a
my heart,
Lord I want to be like Jesus in-a my heart.
—*African American Spiritual, 18th-19th centuries*

Searcher of all hearts, you know my heart, and how
it stands with me. You have made it, you know
whether I love you. All I am or have that has any
goodness in it, I am or have alone through you, for
it is all your work in me; but it must be yours also
by the free surrender of my heart. . . . Gladly would
I devote my whole being to you; accept me, then, as
a living sacrifice, and give me the mind that was in
Christ Jesus, to the glory of God the Father.
—*Johann Michael Sailer, 18th-19th centuries*

Prayers of Reginald Heber, 18th-19th centuries

♦   O Lord Jesus Christ, who (as at this time) did burst
the prison-house of the grave, and open to all that
believe in your name the gate of a glorious resurrec-

tion, let the light of your truth, we beseech you, shine on all that dwell in darkness. Have mercy on the great land of India. Bless all the rulers and peoples of that land. Bless, guide, and enlighten all who are inquiring after truth, and hasten the time, if it be your gracious will, when the knowledge of your name shall cover the world as the waters cover the sea; for the sake of your son, our Lord and Saviour.

◆   Holy, holy, holy! Lord God Almighty!
Early in the morning our song shall rise to you;
Holy, holy, holy! merciful and mighty!
God in three persons, blessed Trinity!
Holy, holy, holy! though the darkness hide you,
Though the eye of sinful man your glory may
    not see;
Only you are holy; there is none beside you,
Perfect in power, in love, and purity.

Now, O God, our Saviour, we entreat you, subdue our iniquities. Only your almighty arm can vanquish them. We look to you for victory. Fight for us, fight in us, that we may be more than conquerors, through him who loved us, even Jesus Christ, our only Lord and Saviour.
—*Edward Bickersteth, 18th-19th centuries*

Come in, O Christ, and judge us; come and cast out for us every sin that hinders you; come purge our souls by your presence. Come be our King forever.

—Phillips Brooks, 19th century

Lord, we pray you bless the work of all missionary societies. Teach us to realize that the command to go into all the world and preach the gospel to every creature is binding in measure to each individual. Show us what we ought to do. Increase our zeal, our interest, our service, our supplications. May we help in sending others, if we cannot go ourselves, by our prayers and offering; for the sake of Jesus Christ our Lord.

—Church Missionary Society, 19th century

Prayers of Thomas Arnold, 19th century

♦ O Lord, save us from idle words, and grant that our hearts may be truly cleansed and filled with your Holy Spirit, and that we may arise to serve you or lie down to sleep in entire confidence in you and submission to your will, ready for life or for death. Let us live for the day, not overcharged with worldly cares, but feeling that our treasure is not here, and desiring truly to be joined to you in your heavenly kingdom and to those who are already gone to you.

◆   O gracious Father, keep us through your Holy
       Spirit; keep our hearts soft and tender now in
       health and amidst the bustle of the world; keep the
       thought of yourself present to us as our Father in
       Jesus Christ; and keep alive in us a spirit of love
       and meekness to all men, that we may be at once
       gentle and active and firm.

My father, help me as a follower of Christ to say,
"Thy will be done." You would not have me accept
your will because I *must*, but because I *may*. You
would have me take it, not with resignation, but
with joy, not with the absence of murmur, but with
the song of praise. How shall I reach this goal? I
shall only reach it by feeling what the psalmist
felt—that your will comes from a "good Spirit,"
and goes towards a "land of uprightness." Teach
me that your will is love; teach me that your love is
wise.
—*George Matheson, 19th century*

Use me then, my Savior, for whatever purpose, and
in whatever way, you may require. Here is my poor
heart, an empty vessel; fill it with your grace. Here
is my sinful and troubled soul; quicken it and
refresh it with your love. Take my heart for your
abode; my mouth to spread abroad the glory of
your name; my love and all my powers, for the advancement of your believing people; and never

allow the steadfastness and confidence of my faith
to abate—that so at all times I may be enabled from
the heart to say, "Jesus needs me, and I Him."
—*Dwight L. Moody, 19th century*

Oh how oft I wake and find
I have been forgetting thee!
I am never from thy mind:
Thou it is that wakest me.
—*George MacDonald, 19th century*

Prayers of Edward Bouverie Pusey, 19th century

◆ Let me not seek [outside] you what I can find only
in you, O Lord, peace and rest and joy and bliss,
which abide only in your abiding joy. Lift up my
soul above the weary round of harassing thoughts
to your eternal presence. Lift up my soul to the
pure, bright, serene, radiant atmosphere of your
presence, that there I may breathe freely, there
repose in your love, there be at rest from myself,
and from all things that weary me; and thence
return, arrayed with your peace, to do and bear
what shall please you.

◆ O Lord, who, in infinite wisdom and love, orders
all things for your children, order everything this
day for me in your tender pity. You know my weakness, who made me; you know how my soul
shrinks from all pain of soul. Lord, I know you will

lay no greater burden on me than you can help
me to bear. Teach me to receive all things this day
from you. Enable me to commend myself in all
things to you; grant me in all things to please
you; bring me through all things nearer unto you;
bring me, day by day, nearer to yourself, to life
everlasting.

◆   Teach me, O Father, how to ask you each moment,
silently, for your help. If I fail, teach me at once to
ask you to forgive me. If I am disquieted, enable
me, by your grace, quickly to turn to you. May
nothing this day come between me and you. . . .

◆   Living or dying, Lord, I would be yours; keep me
your own for ever, and draw me day by day nearer
to yourself, until I be wholly filled with your love,
and fitted to behold you, face to face.

Prayers of William Bright, 19th century

◆   O God, by whom the meek are guided in judgment, and light rises up in darkness for the godly;
grant us, in all our doubts and uncertainties, the
grace to ask what you would have us to do; that
the Spirit of wisdom may save us from all false
choices, and that in your light we may see light,
and in your straight path may not stumble,
through Jesus Christ our Lord.

- O most loving Father, whose will it is for us to give thanks for all things, to dread nothing but the loss of you, and to cast all our care on you who cares for us; preserve us from faithless fears and worldly anxieties, and grant that no clouds of this mortal life may hide from us the light of that love which is immortal, and which you have manifested unto us in your Son, Jesus Christ our Lord.

- O Lord, grant all who contend for the faith, never to injure it by clamor and impatience; but, speaking your precious truth in love, so to present it that it may be loved, and that men may see in it your goodness and beauty.

Prayers of Christina Rossetti, 19th century

- O Lord, with whom are strength and wisdom, put forth your strength, I implore you, for your own sake and for our sakes, and stand up to help us; for we are deceivable and weak persons, frail and brief, unstable and afraid, unless you put the might of your Holy Spirit within us.

- Grant, O Lord, that we may carefully watch over our tempers and every unholy feeling; remove whatever in us may be a stumbling-block in another's way; that, by conforming to your will in small things, we may hope by your protection and help to pass safely through the greater dangers and trials to which we may be exposed.

♦   O Lord, who is as the shadow of a great rock in a weary land, who beholds your weak creatures, weary of labor, weary of pleasure, weary of hope deferred, weary of self, in your abundant compassion and unutterable tenderness, bring us, we pray you, unto your rest.

♦   O my God, by whose loving providence, sorrows, difficulties, trials, dangers, become means of grace, lessons of patience, channels of hope, grant us good will to use and not abuse those our privileges . . .

♦   O Lord, strengthen and support . . . all persons unjustly accused or underrated. Comfort them by the ever-present thought that you know the whole truth, and will, in your own good time, make their righteousness as clear as the light. Give them grace to pray for such as do them wrong, and hear and bless them when they pray; for the sake of Jesus Christ our Lord and Savior.

My life, my all, Lord, I entreat
Take, and use, and make replete
With the love and patience sweet
That made *your* life so complete.
—*Mary Slessor, 19th century*

Prayers of Rowland Williams, 19th century

♦ Lord, let your holy breath ever keep alive in us that fire which your son of old came to kindle upon earth, that we also may be anointed with the spirit of peace, holiness, and obedience, and dwell in your fellowship forever.

♦ Lord . . . From all perplexity of mind; from loneliness of thought, and discontented brooding; from wondering what you would have us do, deliver us, Lord. Especially from whatever sin besets us, save and deliver us with might, O Lord.

Prayers of James Martineau, 19th century

♦ O God . . . we have been slow to the calls of affection, heedless of the duties, hard under the sorrows, which are your gracious discipline; yet are oppressed with cares you lay not on us, with ease you do not permit, and wants you will never bless. Visit us with the wrestlings of your Spirit: and lay on us the cross, if we may but grow into the holiness of Christ.

♦ O God, our everlasting hope! . . . Every work of our hand may we do unto you; in every trouble, trace some lights of yours; and let no blessing fall on dry and thankless hearts. . . . Fill us with patient tenderness for others, seeing that we also are in the same case before you; and make us ready to help, and quick to forgive. And then, fix every grace, compose every fear, by a steady trust in your eternal realities.

♦ Prepare us to seek our rest, not in outward ease, but in inward devotedness, only fulfil to us the word of the chief of saints, leave us his peace while we remain here, and then receive us unto yourself to mingle with the mighty company of our forerunners; through Jesus Christ our Lord.

Prayers of Henry Alford, 19th century

♦ May we never presume upon your protection when we are forsaking your paths and tempting you. May we never, for the sake of any supposed gain or advancement, quench the testimony of your Spirit, or prove disloyal to your service. Do so support us in all temptations that, when we have been tried, we may receive the crown of life, which you have prepared for them that love you.

♦ O Lord . . . may we learn to love you whom we have not seen, by loving our brothers and sisters whom we have seen. Teach us, O heavenly Father, the love by which you have loved us; fashion us, O blessed Lord, after your own example of love; shed abroad, O Holy Spirit of love, the love of God . . . in our hearts.

Our Father, grant us, this day, the sense of your presence to cheer, and your light to direct us, and give us strength for your service. And yet more, Father, give us your own help and blessing in our sorrows, our faintness, our failure and sin. You know that we cannot bear our burdens alone. We are only little children, and the world seems very dark to us, and our path very hard, if we are alone. But we are your little children; and so we know we can come to our father, to ask you to help us, and enliven us, and strengthen us, and give us hope. We are not ashamed of our tears, for our Lord has wept with us. We do not ask you to take away our sorrow, for he was made perfect through suffering; but we do ask you to be with us as you were with him, our Father, close to your little ones, even as he has promised us.

Amen.

—*The Altar at Rome, 19th century*

Prayers of John Henry Newman, 19th century

♦ Visit me not, O my loving Lord—if it be not wrong so to pray—visit me not with those trying visitations which saints alone can bear! Pity my weakness, and lead me heavenwards in a safe and tranquil course. Still I leave all in your hands— only, if you shall bring heavier trials on me, give me more grace, flood me with the fulness of your strength and consolation.

♦   Dear God, our entire lives have been journeys of
mercies and blessings shown to those most unde-
serving of them. Year after year you have carried us
on, removed dangers from our paths, refreshed us,
been patient with us, directed us, sustained us. O,
don't leave us when we are weak and faithless. We
know you will stay with us, that we can rest as-
sured in you. As we are true to your ways, you
will, to the very end, be superabundantly good to
us. We may rest upon your arm; we can sleep like
babies in their mothers' laps.

The day returns and brings us the petty round of
irritating concerns and duties. Help us to . . . perform them with laughter and kind faces, let cheer-
fulness abound with industry. Enable us to go
blithely on our business all this day, bring us to our
resting beds weary and content and undishonored,
and grant us in the end the gift of sleep.
—*Robert Louis Stevenson, 19th century*

Prayers of William Booth, 19th century

♦   O God, you know our desperate need for your gift
of understanding and forgiveness in order to live
in harmony with our neighbors. You know how
repeatedly and how hopelessly we forget your love
for us, and turn back continually to ourselves as
though your love were not to be trusted. We con-

fess that we have nourished grievances and irritations which we ought to forgive; we have sinfully thought our differences too great for reconciliation; and our community is wounded by our selfishness, prejudice, and pride. . . . Since you are love, and the source of all love, give us strength to leave the easy path of self-satisfaction; grant us the courage to forgive as we hope to be forgiven; and in your mercy heal our divisions and make us whole, together, in the love which we have from you; through Jesus Christ our Lord.

♦ Lord, give to all these people who have authority over others the wisdom to govern well, and the grace to know in their hearts that nothing is firm that is not just, and that the test of justice is to turn people from following after evil, to seek what is good.

Prayers of St. Therese of Lisieux, 19th century

♦ My God, I choose the whole lot. No point in becoming a saint by halves. I'm not afraid of suffering for your sake; the only thing I'm afraid of is clinging to my own will. Take it, I want the whole lot, everything whatsoever that is your will for me.

♦ O my God, you have surpassed all I have hoped for, and I want to sing of your mercies.

Prayers of Charles Haddon Spurgeon, 19th century

♦ O Lord Jesus, our souls fly to you. You are the only refuge of our heart. Our confidence is fixed upon your blood and righteousness, and we believe that these will never fail us. We are persuaded that if we build upon this Rock of ages, the floods may come, and the winds may beat upon that house, but it shall not fall because it is built upon the rock. Renew the faith of your people. Let its former simplicity come back. May we each of us come to Jesus as we did at first—weary, and overworn, and sad, and sinful—and find in him all that our largest want can possibly demand. Oh for grace today to take a bleeding Savior at his word, and to believe him to be the propitiation for our sins.

♦ Lord God, sacred Trinity, Father, Son, and Holy Ghost, reign on earth. Let your eternal purposes be accomplished. Let the decrees of your sovereignty be carried out. Let your grace be glorified. Let the whole earth be filled with your glory. We know no deeper and no higher prayer than this; oh, that it were fulfilled right speedily!

O God, since you are Love, and he that loves not you and his brethren knows you not, and abides in death, deliver us from injustice, envy, hatred, and malice; give us grace to pardon all who have offended us, and to bear with one another, even as you, Lord, bear with us, in your patience and great lovingkindness.

—*Eugene Bersier, 19th century*

Almighty God, we earnestly ask you to look upon this household. Grant that every member of it may be taught and guided of you. Bless the relations and friends of each of us. You know their several necessities. Prosper . . . every effort at home and abroad to advance your kingdom; through Jesus Christ our Lord.

—*Archibald Campbell Tait, 19th century*

Prayers of Thomas Thellusson Carter, 19th century

♦ We commend to your lovingkindness, O God, all our relations and friends, that they may be filled with your grace. Have mercy on all sick and dying persons, all who are suffering or in sorrow, and grant to all who are living in error, or ignorance, or sin, the grace of repentance; through Jesus Christ our Lord.

♦ O blessed Jesus . . . we humbly ask you so to dispose the hearts of all kings, princes, and governors of this world, that by your inspiration they may rule in righteousness, and labor for the well-being of the people committed to them. Prosper and bless all who are striving to do your will, that, having faithfully ministered before you, they may receive the recompense of your reward; who, with the Father and Holy

Ghost, lives and reigns, one God, world without
end.

O our God, we would not hide our daily shortcom-
ings from you. Oh! forgive us in Christ. Our Father,
never let us be without the indwelling of your Holy
Spirit for an hour. Let our lives be every day more
unconscious of our own presence and more con-
scious of yours. Make us instruments in your hand
for advancing your kingdom, and for uniting all
Christians in this land; for the sake of him who
loved us, and died for us, even Jesus Christ.
—*Norman Macleod, 19th century*

O you, Lord of all worlds, we bless your name for
all those who have entered into their rest, and
reached the Promised Land, where you are seen
face to face. Give us grace to follow in their
footsteps, as they followed in the footsteps of your
holy Son. Encourage our wavering hearts by their
example, and help us to see in them the memorials
of your redeeming grace, and pledges of the
heavenly might in which the weak are made
strong. Keep alive in us the memory of those dear
to ourselves, whom you have called out of this
world, and make it powerful to subdue within us
every vile and unworthy thought. Grant that every
remembrance that turns our hearts from things
seen to things unseen, may lead us always up-

wards to you, till we too come to the eternal rest
that you have prepared for your people; through
Jesus Christ our Lord.
—*Fenton John Anthony Hort, 19th century*

Almighty and everlasting God, lover of peace and
concord, who has called us in Christ to love and
unity, we pray you so rule our hearts by your Holy
Spirit, that we, being delivered by the true fear of
God from all fear of people, may evermore serve
you in righteousness, mercy, humility, and gentle-
ness towards each other.
—*Christian C.J. Bunsen, 19th century*

O Saviour Christ, our woes dispel
for some are sick and some are sad;
And some have never loved you well,
and some have lost the love they had.
Your touch has still its ancient power
No word from you can fruitless fall;
Here in this joyful worship hour
And in your mercy, heal us all.
—*Henry Twells, 19th century*

Grant, O merciful God, that with malice toward
none, with charity to all, with firmness in the right
as you give us to see the right, we may strive to
finish the work we are in; to bind up the nation's

wounds; to care for him who shall have borne the
battle and for his widow and his orphan; to do all
which may achieve and cherish a just and lasting
peace among ourselves and with all nations.
—*Abraham Lincoln, 19th century*

O holy Savior, friend unseen,
since on your arm you bidd'st me lean,
Help me throughout life's changing scene,
by faith to cling to you.
Though faith and hope are often tried,
I ask not, need not aught beside;
So safe, so calm, so satisfied,
the soul that clings to you.
Blest is my lot, whatever befall;
What can disturb me, who appall,
While as my Strength, my Rock, my All,
Savior, I cling to you?
—*Charlotte Elliott, 19th century*

Prayers of Frances Ridley Havergal, 19th century

♦   Take my life, and let it be
Consecrated, Lord, to thee.
Take my moments and my days,
Let them flow in ceaseless praise.
Take my hands, and let them move
At the impulse of thy love.
Take my feet, and let them be

Swift and "beautiful" for thee.
Take my voice, and let me sing
Always, only, for my King.
Take my lips, and let them be
Filled with messages from thee.
Take my silver and my gold,
Not a mite would I withhold.
Take my intellect, and use
Every power as thou shalt choose.
Take my will, and make it thine;
It shall be no longer mine.
Take my heart, it *is* thine own;
It shall be thy royal throne.

◆   What know we, Holy God, of thee,
　　Thy being and thine essence pure?
Too bright the very mystery
　　For mortal vision to endure.
We only know thy word sublime,
　　Thou art a Spirit! Perfect! One!
Unlimited by space or time,
　　Unknown but through the eternal Son.
By change untouched, by thought untraced,
　　And by created eye unseen,
In thy great Present is embraced
　　All that shall be, all that hath been.
O Father of our spirits, now
　　We seek Thee in our Savior's face;
In truth and spirit we would bow,
　　And worship where we cannot trace.

Blessed Lord, by whose providence all Holy Scriptures were written and preserved for our instruction, give us grace to study them this and every day, with patience and love. Strengthen our souls with the fulness of their divine teaching. Keep from us all pride and irreverence. Guide us in the deep things of your heavenly wisdom, and of your great mercy lead us by your word unto everlasting life; through Jesus Christ our Lord and Saviour.
—*Brooke Foss Westcott, 19th century*

O Lord, the hard-won miles
  have worn my stumbling feet:
Oh, soothe me with thy smiles,
  And make my life complete.
The thorns were thick and keen
  Where'er I trembling trod;
The way was long between
  My wounded feet and God.
Where healing waters flow
  Do thou my footsteps lead.
My heart is aching so;
  Thy gracious balm I need.
—*Paul Dunbar, 19th century*

Gracious Lord, who was born of a woman, who accepted the ministry of women, and who took into your arms little children to bless them, be present, we pray you, with the women who now minister for you to their sisters in heathen and Moslem countries; and be with all those to whom you have given the care of children to be brought up in your fear and love. By means of these your servants raise the women of these lands to know and enjoy the blessing and honor that are in your purpose for women, and so give your Word that great may be the company of the women who labor in the Lord, and carry into darkened homes the light of your presence and the joy of your peace; hear us for your name's sake.

—*Church Missionary Society, 19th century*

Prayers of Walter Rauschenbusch, 19th-20th centuries

◆   (for employers): . . . Amid the numberless irritations and anxieties of their position, help them to keep a quiet and patient temper . . . Since they hold power over the bread, the safety, and the hopes of the workers, may they wield their powers justly and with love . . .

◆   (for people in business): . . . As long as man is set against man in a struggle for wealth, help the men in business to make their contest, as far as may be, a test of excellence, by which even the defeated may be spurred to better work . . . Establish in unshaken fidelity all who hold in trust the savings of others . . . cause them to realize that they serve not themselves alone, but hold high public functions,

and do save them from betraying the interests of
the many for their own enrichment, lest a new
tyranny grow up in a land that is dedicated to
freedom. . . .

♦   (for artists and musicians): . . . We praise you for
our brothers and sisters, the masters of form and
color and sound, who have power to unlock for us
the vaster spaces of emotion and to lead us by their
hand into the reaches of nobler passions. We rejoice
in their gifts and pray you to save them from the
temptations which beset their powers. Save them
from the discouragements of a selfish ambition and
from the vanity that feeds on cheap applause, from
the snare of the senses and from the dark phantoms
that haunt the listening soul. . .

♦   (for judges): . . . As they deduce the principles
which underlie the customary laws of men and
women, give unto them the larger vision of the
reign of law and the ordered universe, of the prece-
dents of nature and providence, and allow them
not to forget or to be ignorant of those inevitable
laws of yours which outlive the lives of people. . . .
Cause them to be the servants of all men, but the
hirelings of none. . . .

♦   (for lawyers and legislators): . . . Grant to all
lawyers a deep consciousness that they are called
of God to see justice done, and that they prostitute
a holy duty if ever they connive in its defeat. Fill

them with a high determination to make the courts of our land a strong fortress of defense for the poor and weak, and never a castle of oppression for the hard and cunning. . . .

♦   (for doctors and nurses): . . . Though they deal with the frail human body, may they have an abiding sense of the eternal value of the life residing in it, that by the call of faith and hope they may summon to their aid the mysterious human spirit and the powers of your all-pervading life.
—*adapted*

♦   (for writers and journalists): . . . Inspire them with a determined love for honest work and a staunch hatred for the making of lies, lest the judgments of our nation be perverted and we be taught to call light darkness and darkness light. Since the sanity and wisdom of a nation are in their charge, may they count it shame to set the baser passions of people on fire for the sake of gain. May they never suffer themselves to be used in drugging the mind of the people with falsehood and prejudice. . . .

♦   (for ministers): . . . Free us from all entanglements that have hushed our voice and bound our action. Grant us grace to look upon the veiled sins of the rich and the coarse vices of the poor through your eyes. . . . Make us faithful shepherds of your flock, true seers of God, and true followers of Jesus.

- (for teachers): . . . Grant them an abiding consciousness that they are coworkers with you, great
teacher of humanity, and that you have charged
them with the holy duty of bringing forth from the
budding life of the young the mysterious stores of
character and ability which you have hidden in
them. . . .

- (for mothers): . . . Widen their vision that they may
see themselves, not as the mothers of one child
alone, but as the patriot women of their nation,
who alone can build up the better future with fresh
and purer life. . . .

- (for our city): . . . Help us to make our city the
mighty common workshop of our people, where
everyone will find his place and task . . . keen to do
his best with hand and mind. Help us to make our
city the greater home of our people, where all may
live their lives in comfort, unafraid, loving their
loves in peace and rounding out their years in
strength. . . .

- (for the world): . . . We praise you for the arching
sky and the blessed winds, for the driving clouds
and the constellations on high. We praise you for
the salt sea and the running water, for the everlasting hills, for the trees, and for the grass under our
feet. We thank you for our senses by which we can
see the splendor of the morning, and hear the

jubilant songs of love, and smell the breath of the springtime. Grant us, we pray you, a heart wide open to all this joy and beauty, and save our souls from being so steeped in care or so darkened by passion that we pass heedless and unseeing when even the thornbush by the wayside is aflame with the glory of God.

Prayers of William Temple, 19th-20th centuries

♦ O God our judge and savior, set before us the vision of your purity and let us see our sins in the light of your countenance; pierce our self-contentment with the shafts of your burning love and let that love consume in us all that hinders us from perfect service of your cause; for as your holiness is our judgment, so are your wounds our salvation.

♦ O Lord Jesus Christ, word and revelation of the eternal Father, come, we pray you, take possession of our hearts and reign where you have right to reign. So fill our minds with your thought and our imaginations with the picture of your love, that there may be in us no room for any desire that is discordant with your holy will. Cleanse us, we pray you, from all that may make us deaf to your call or slow to obey it, who, with the Father and the Holy Spirit are one God, blessed for ever.

Prayers of Richard Meux Benson, 19th-20th centuries

◆   Bless, O Lord, our soldiers and sailors, of whatever rank or quality. Grant that in the midst of every temptation which besets them they may fight manfully against the world, the flesh, and the devil; and, resisting all evil by the spirit of your . . . strength, may acquire true courage in the victory of faith. Prosper them in the maintenance of our country's honor, and keep them safe from enemies spiritual and temporal, that they may glorify you upon the earth, until they are called to rest in the triumph of your glory; through Jesus Christ our Lord.

◆   O blessed Savior, who was pleased yourself to be reckoned among the craftsmen, bless all those who labor with their hands, that their work may be done for your honor and rewarded with your approval; for your own name's sake.

Prayers of John Henry Jowett, 19th-20th centuries

◆   O God our Father, we would thank you for all the bright things of life. Help us to see them, and to count them, and to remember them, that our lives may flow in ceaseless praise; for the sake of Christ Jesus our Lord.

◆   Our Father, teach us not only your will, but how to do it. Teach us the best way of doing the best thing,

lest we spoil the end by unworthy means; for the
sake of Christ Jesus our Lord.

O Lord, if this I am now going through is the right
road home, then I will not murmur!
—*Rosalind Goforth, 19th-20th centuries*

I am thine, O Lord, I have heard thy voice,
And it told thy love to me;
but I long to rise in the arms of faith
and be closer drawn to thee.
Consecrate me now to thy service, Lord,
by the power of grace divine;
Let my soul look up with a steadfast hope,
and my will be lost in thine.
O, the pure delight of a single hour
that before thy throne I spend,
When I kneel in prayer, and with you, my God,
I commune as friend with friend!
There are depths of love that I cannot know
till I cross the narrow sea;
There are heights of joy that I may not reach
till I rest in peace with thee.
—*Fanny J. Crosby, 19th-20th centuries*

For the beauty of the earth,
For the beauty of the sky,
For the love which from our birth

Over and around us lies,
Lord of all, to thee we raise
This our joyful hymn of praise.
For the joy of human love,
Brother, sister, parent, child,
Friends on earth, and friends above,
For all gentle thoughts and mild,
Lord of all, to thee we raise
This our joyful hymn of praise.
—*Folliott Sandford Pierpoint, 19th-20th centuries*

From silken self, O Captain free
Thy soldier, who would follow Thee:
From subtle love of softening things,
From easy choices, weakenings,
From all that dims Thy Calvary,
O Lamb of God, deliver me.
—*Amy Carmichael, 19th-20th centuries*

Prayers of Evelyn Underhill, 19th-20th centuries

◆   Teach me a proper reverence for all that unformed
       human nature on which your Holy Spirit rests,
       which you can penetrate, transform, make holy,
       and in which you show to us the very glory of the
       only-begotten of the Father, full of grace and truth.

◆   Show me what the attachments and cravings are,
       which hold me down below your level of total self-
       surrender, real love. Show me the things that lum-

ber up my heart, so that it cannot be filled with your life and power. What are they? People? Ambitions? Interests? Comforts? Anxieties? Self-chosen aims?

♦   Take from me all that hinders and teach me to accept in its place all that you accept: the ceaseless demands, needs, conflicts, pressures, misunderstandings even of those who love you best.

♦   Help me to discern the particular price you ask and help me to pay the particular price—whatever it may be.

Almighty God, guide of the years that are past, and hope of the years to come, accept the service of the hearts and minds of all Members of this body "in order to form a more perfect union, establish justice, insure domestic tranquility, provide for the common defense, promote the general welfare, and secure the blessings of liberty to ourselves and our posterity." To this end will you remove every barrier which separates man from man, class from class, race from race, and fuse us into one mighty body—heart to heart, mind to mind, soul to soul, strong in the Lord and in the power of his might. In the redeemer's name. Amen.
—*opening prayer for the United States Senate, March of 1969*

O you who was, and are, and are to come, I thank
you that this Christian way on which I walk is no
untried or uncharted road, but a road beaten hard
by the footsteps of saints, apostles, prophets, and
martyrs. I thank you for the finger-posts and
danger-signals with which it is marked at every
turning and which may be known to me through
the study of the Bible and of all history, and of all
the great literature of the world. Beyond all I give
you devout and humble thanks for the great gift of
Jesus Christ, the pioneer of our faith. . . and that I
am not called upon to face any temptation or trial
which he did not first endure. Forbid it, Holy Lord,
that I should fail to profit by these great memories
of the ages that are gone by . . . through Jesus
Christ my Lord.
—*John Baillie, 19th-20th centuries*

The water that I live in
is full of piranha
and it doesn't do
to have a bleeding heart
in this locality.
Please God
get me out of this water
or give me a shell
or teeth . . .
Just don't leave me here
with nothing
but the conviction

that piranha
are all God's children
too.
—*Evangeline Paterson, 20th century*

God, if there be a God, if you will prove to me
that you are, and if you will give me peace, I will
give you my whole life. I'll do anything you ask
me to do, go where you send me, obey you all my
days.
—*Isobel Kuhn, 20th century*

How easy for me to live with you, O Lord!
How easy for me to believe in you!
When my mind parts in bewilderment or falters,
when the most intelligent people see no further
than this day's end
and do not know what must be done tomorrow,
You grant me the serene certitude
that you exist and that you will take care
that not all the paths of good be closed.
Atop the ridge of earthly fame,
I look back in wonder at the path
which I alone could never have found,
a wondrous path through despair to this point
from which I, too, could transmit to mankind
a reflection of your rays.
And as much as I must still reflect
You will give me.

But as much as I cannot take up
You will have already assigned to others.
—*Aleksandr Solzhenitsyn, 20th century*

O heavenly Father, I praise and thank you
For the peace of the night,
I praise and thank you for this new day.
I praise and thank you for all your goodness
and faithfulness throughout my life.
You have granted me many blessings:
Now let me accept tribulation
from your hand.
You will not lay on me more
than I can bear.
You make all things work together for good
for your children.
—*Dietrich Bonhoeffer, 20th century*

You take the pen,
and the lines dance.
You take the flute,
and the notes shimmer.
You take the brush,
and the colours sing.
So all things have meaning and beauty
in that space beyond time where you are.
How, then, can I hold back anything from you?
—*Dag Hammarskjold, 20th century*

Prayers of Howard Thurman, 20th century

♦   Give me the listening ear. I seek this day the ear that
        will not shrink from the word that corrects and ad-
        monishes—the word that holds up before me the
        image of myself that causes me to pause and recon-
        sider—the word that challenges me to deeper con-
        secration and higher resolve—the word that lays bare
        needs that make my own days uneasy, that seizes
        upon every good decent impulse of my nature, chan-
        neling it into paths of healing in the lives of others. . . .

        Give me this day—the eye that is willing to see the
        meaning of the ordinary, the familiar, the com-
        monplace—the eye that is willing to see my own
        faults for what they are—the eye that is willing to
        see the likable qualities in those I may not like—the
        mistake in what I thought was correct—the
        strength in what I had labeled as weakness. Give
        me the eye that is willing to see that you have not
        left yourself without a witness in every living
        thing. Thus to walk with reverence and sensitivity
        through all the days of my life.
        Give me the listening ear
        The eye that is willing to see.

♦   Be in the fleeting word, our Father, the stumbling
        effort. Touch mind and heart and life, that as we
        move from this place into the way that we must
        take, we shall not be alone, but shall feel your
        presence beside us, all the way.

Prayers of Peter Marshall, 20th century

◆   Give to us more faith. We have so little . . . we say.
      Yet we have faith in each other—in checks and
      banks, in trains and airplanes, in cooks, and in
      strangers who drive us in cabs. Forgive us for our
      stupidity, that we have faith in people whom we do
      not know, and are so reluctant to have faith in you
      who knows us altogether.

◆   Forbid it, Lord, that our roots become too firmly at-
      tached to this earth, that we should fall in love with
      things.

◆   Help us to understand that the pilgrimage of this
      life is but an introduction, a preface, a training
      school for what is to come. Then shall we see all of
      life in its true perspective. Then shall we not fall in
      love with the things of time, but come to love the
      things that endure. Then shall we be saved from
      the tyranny of possessions which we have no
      leisure to enjoy, of property whose care becomes a
      burden. Give us, we pray, the courage to simplify
      our lives.

◆   So may we be mature in our faith, childlike but
      never childish, humble but never cringing, under-
      standing but never conceited. So help us, O God, to
      live and not merely to exist, that we may have joy
      in our work. In your name, who alone can give us

moderation and balance and zest for living, we pray.

We commend to you, Almighty God, the whole Christian Church in the world. Bless all in every place who call on the name of our Lord Jesus Christ. May the grace and power of the Holy Ghost fill every member, so that the whole company of your faithful people may bear witness for you on the earth. Look in mercy on the errors and confusions of our time, and be pleased amidst them to speak your own peace, and to draw the hearts of Christians everywhere nearer to the Lord Jesus Christ. If it be good in your sight, heal the outward divisions of your people, disposing all Christian hearts to a true union of order in the truth, for the work of the one Lord. But above all things we ask you for the unity of the Holy Spirit, that we may all be one in the Father and in the Son; to the glory of your name through Jesus Christ our Lord.

—*H.C.G. Moule, 20th century*

Listen, Lord,
a mother's praying
low and quiet:
listen, please.
Listen what her tears

are saying,
see her heart
upon its knees;
lift the load
from her bowed shoulders
till she sees
and understands,
You, Who hold
the worlds together,
hold her problems
in Your hands.
—*Ruth Bell Graham, 20th century*

Prayers of Mother Teresa of Calcutta, 20th century

◆   Eternal life, Father, is to know you, the one true
        God, and Jesus Christ, whom you have sent.

        May we bring this eternal life to the poor, deprived
        as they are of all comfort, of material possessions;
        may they come to know you, love you, possess
        you, share in your life, you who are the God and
        Father of men and of my Lord Jesus Christ, source
        of all truth and goodness and happiness.

◆   My Lord, I love You.
        My God, I am sorry.
        My God, I believe in You.
        My God, I trust You.
        Help us to love one another
        as You love us.

God, I pray, light these idle sticks of my life and may I burn for you. Consume my life, my God, for it is yours. I seek not a long life, but a full one, like you, Lord Jesus.

—*Jim Elliot, 20th century*

Biographical Information

Alcuin (d. 804). Scholar, abbot of monastery St. Martin of Tours; influential in revision of Vulgate text of the Bible.

Alford, Henry (1810-1871). Dean of Canterbury, hymnwriter ("Come ye thankful people, come"); published edition of New Testament 1849-61.

Alfred the Great (849-899). King of Wessex from 871; responsible for the preservation and translation of many Christian, philosophical, and historical writings.

Ambrose, St. (c. 339-397). Bishop of Milan, famous preacher, teacher, and helper of the poor; influenced Augustine.

Andrewes, Lancelot (1555-1626). Bishop of Winchester from 1619; well-known preacher and church leader.

Anselm, St. (1033-1109). Archbishop of Canterbury from 1093; Christian scholar and writer.

Aquinas, St. Thomas (1224-1274). Theologian and philosopher; wrote extensively, greatly influencing both Catholic and Protestant traditions.

Arndt, Johann (1555-1621). German Lutheran mystic and writer.

Arnold, Thomas (1795-1842). Anglican teacher and minister.

Augustine, St. (354-430). Bishop of Hippo, "greatest of the Latin fathers"; philosopher, apologist.

Bacon, Francis (1561-1626). Philosopher, essayist, and lawyer.

Baillie, John (1886-1960). Scottish theologian, writer, and apologist.

Barrow, Isaac (1630-1677). Mathematician and Anglican clergyman.

Basil, St. (the Great) (c. 329-379). Bishop, ascetic, and teacher.

Becon, Thomas (c. 1512-1567). English Reformer and writer.

Beethoven, Ludwig von (1770-1827). German composer of the Romantic era.

Benson, Richard Meux (1824-1915). Founder of the Society of St. John the Evangelist, an Anglican community of mission priests and laymen.

Bernard of Clairvaux, St. (1090-1153). Monastic reformer, mystic, and theologian.

Bernardine, St. (1380-1444). Franciscan friar and reformer.

Bersier, Eugene (1831-1889). Swiss pastor, leader of Free Reformed Church.

Bickersteth, Edward (1786-1850). English Evangelical clergyman and writer.

Bonhoeffer, Dietrich (1906-1945). German Lutheran pastor, writer; imprisoned and executed for his opposition to Hitler.

Book of Common Prayer (since 1544, several revisions). Official service book of the Church of England.

Booth, William (1829-1912). Founder and first general of the Salvation Army.

Bradstreet, Anne (1612-1672). Puritan housewife, mother, and poet.

Bridget, St. (c. 455-c. 523). Patron saint of pity and mercy; inspired convent system in Ireland.

Bright, William (1824-1901). Scholar and hymnwriter.

Brooks, Phillips (1835-1893). American preacher and bishop, rector of Boston's Holy Trinity Church; he wrote the Christmas carol "O little town of Bethelem."

Bunsen, Christian C.J. (1791-1860). Theologian and Prussian diplomat.

Byzantine (from 5th century). Refers to Eastern Orthodox Church, including the four ancient patriarchal districts of Constantinople, Alexandria, Antioch, and Jerusalem.

Calvin, John (1509-1564). French Reformer and theologian; his *Institutes* are the basis of Calvinism.

Carmichael, Amy (1867-1951). Poet and missionary to India.

Carter, Thomas Thellusson (1808-1901). Founded a House of Mercy for "fallen women" and later a sisterhood, the Community of St. John the Baptist, to carry on that ministry.

Catherine of Siena, St. (1347-1380). Dominican nun, known for her letters on many subjects.

Chrysostom, St. John, (c. 344/354-407). Bishop of Constantinople; named "golden-mouthed" for his preaching, a writer.

Church Missionary Society (founded 1799). First major evangelical mission organization of the Church of England.

Clement of Rome, St. (fl. c. 90-100). Prominent church leader; some of his letters to churches received almost scriptural status.

Coke, Thomas (1747-1814). Methodist preacher; worked with John Wesley, superintendent of Methodist missions.

Cosin, John (1594-1672). Bishop of Durham, wrote *Collection of Private Devotions*.

Coverdale, Miles (1483-1546). Augustinian monk and later Puritan leader; produced in 1535 the first complete English translation of the Bible.

Cowper, William (1731-1800). English poet (translated Homer) and prominent hymnwriter.

Crosby, Fanny J. (Mrs. F.J. Van Alstyne) (1823-1915). Blind American hymnwriter ("To God Be the Glory").

Cyril, St. (d. 444). Patriarch of Alexandria, prolific writer on theology.

***Didache* (1st, 2nd, or 3rd century).** Greek handbook of instructions in morals and church order, probably considered by some early believers to be of scriptural status.

Dionysius the Great (d. c. 264). Bishop of Alexandria, pupil of Origen, theologian.

Doddridge, Philip (1702-1751). Teacher of ministers; hymnwriter.

Donne, John (1573-1631). English poet whose works were considered to be spiritual/mystical in nature.

Dunbar, Paul (1872-1906). American author.

Egbert (d. 766). Archbishop of York, teacher (taught Alcuin).

Egyptian liturgy, of Jacobites (4th-6th centuries). Originally out of the Antioch (Syrian) branch of the church in the East; named after an early leader.

Elliot, Jim (1927-1956). Missionary to Ecuador; killed by Auca tribesmen.

Elliott, Charlotte (1789-1871). English hymnwriter.

Ephraem the Syrian, St. (c. 306-373). Great classical writer of the Syrian church; poet, hymnwriter, theologian.

Erasmus, Desiderius (c. 1466-1536). Writer and philosopher who sought church reform through scholarship and study of Christ's teachings; some considered him a forerunner of Luther.

Fenelon, Francois Mothe (1651-1715). French ecclesiastic of Jesuit training, missionary.

Francis of Assissi, St. (1182-1226). Founder of the Franciscan Order.

Gelasian Sacramentary (from mid-8th century). Refers to either a particular manuscript or a category of manuscripts, not necessarily connected to Pope Gelasius. The Vatican manuscript by this name dates from the middle of the 8th century.

Goforth, Rosalind (1864-1942). Missionary to China.

Gothic missal (10th-15th centuries). Ceremony of the Mass used in Medieval times.

Graham, Ruth Bell (1920-   ). American author; wife of evangelist Billy Graham.

Gregory, St. (Gregory I) (540-604). Pope from 590, considered one of the four great doctors of Rome in moral theology; preserved ancient literature; wrote and taught extensively.

Grindal, Edmund (1519?-1583). Archbishop of Canterbury from 1575; sought reformation in church government.

Hammarskjold, Dag (1905-1961). Swedish diplomat and writer, secretary-general of the United Nations 1953-1961.

Havergal, Frances Ridley (1838-1879). English poet and hymn-writer.

Heber, Reginald (1783-1826). Bishop of Calcutta and hymnwriter; supported mission work in India.

Henry, Matthew (1662-1714). Biblical expositor; best known for seven-volume *Commentary on the Bible*.

Herbert, George (1593-1633). English poet and pastor.

Hilary of Poitiers, St. (c. 315-368). Bishop of Poitiers; convictions on theological issues (such as his opposition to civil intervention in matters of faith) led to banishment.

Hort, Fenton John Anthony (1828-1892). New Testament Bible scholar; helped edit Greek New Testament which became basis of English Revised Version.

Ignatius of Loyola, St. (1491/5-1556). Founder of the Jesuits.

Innocent III (1160-1216). "One of the greatest popes of the Middle Ages"; many of his decrees and councils shaped church policy for centuries.

Irenaeus, St. (fl. c. 175-c. 195). Bishop of Lyons; wrote several volumes dealing with Gnostic heresies.

Jenks, Benjamin. No information available.

Jerome, St. (c. 345-c. 419). Leading biblical scholar of his day; translated the Bible into language of the common people.

Johnson, Samuel (1709-1784). Author and lexicographer (writer/compiler of dictionaries).

Jowett, John Henry (1864-1923). English Congregationalist preacher; wrote many devotional books.

Julian of Norwich (c. 1342-after 1413). English mystic.

Ken, Thomas (1637-1711). Bishop and writer of hymns and devotions.

Kepler, Johann (1571-1630). A founder of modern astronomy, student of theology.

Knox, John (c. 1514-1572). Scottish Reformer who wrote the Scottish Confession that abolished the Pope's authority in Scotland.

Kuhn, Isobel (1901-1957). Missionary to China.

Leofric (11th century). Bishop of Exeter.

Leonine Sacramentary (7th century). Earliest surviving book of Mass prayers according to the Roman rite.

Lincoln, Abraham (1809-1865). Sixteenth president of the United States; in office during the Civil War and responsible for the abolition of slavery.

Liturgy of St. James (5th century or earlier). Tradition attributes this service to St. James, the brother of Jesus. It is sometimes used in the Orthodox Church.

Liturgy of St. Mark (2nd-5th centuries). Traditional Greek Eucharistic Liturgy of the Church of Alexandria.

Lull, Raymond (c. 1232-1316). Franciscan missionary, mystic, and scholar; one of the first missionaries to the Muslims of Arabia.

Luther, Martin (1483-1546). Founder of the German Reformation; theologian, teacher, and hymnwriter.

MacDonald, George (1824-1905). Scottish pastor and writer.

Macleod, Norman (1812-1872). Scottish minister; friend and adviser to Queen Victoria.

Marshall, Peter (1902-1949). Presbyterian minister; chaplain to the U.S. Senate from 1947.

Martineau, James (1805-1900). English Unitarian minister and teacher; attempted to harmonize religion and "modern thought" of Victorian era; supported temperance movement.

Martyn, Henry (1781-1812). Anglican missionary to India; produced substantial biblical translation work in Hindustani, Persian, and Arabic.

Matheson, George (1842-1906). Scottish minister and hymnwriter ("O Love that wilt not let me go").

Mechthild of Magdeburg, St. (c. 1212-c. 1280). German mystic; her "strong individualism and poetic qualities distinguish her from most mystics."

Melancthon, Philip (1497-1560). Protestant Reformer, professor of Greek at Wittenberg who was influenced by Luther and later led Reformation movement when Luther was in confinement; largely responsible for the Augsburg Confession.

Moody, Dwight L. (1837-1899). American evangelist and founder of the Moody Bible Institute in Chicago; his preaching campaigns set a pattern for the mass rallies and crusades of future evangelists.

More, Sir Thomas (1478-1535). Lord Chancellor of England whose home became a center of intellectual exchange, frequented by Erasmus and other thinkers of the day.

Moule, Handley Carr Glyn (1841-1920). First principal of Ridley Hall, an evangelical theology college within Cambridge; Moule was a major influence for Evangelicalism there.

Mozarabic (6th-8th centuries). Refers to liturgies used in the Iberian Peninsula from earliest times until the 11th century, when Christians took Spain from the Moslems and replaced the Mozarabic with Roman liturgies.

Nerses, St. (Narses the Great) (c. 326-373). Patriarch of Armenia; built schools, hospitals, and sent out monks on evangelical preaching missions.

Newman, John Henry (1801-1890). Tract writer of the Oxford Movement; his sermons and writings had great influence on both the Church of England and the Roman Catholic Church.

Norden, J. No information available.

Parker, Matthew (1504-1575). Archbishop of Canterbury from 1559.

Pascal, Blaise (1623-1662). Mathematician, physicist, inventor, and religious thinker; wrote but did not complete *Apology for the Christian Religion*.

Paterson, Evangeline (1928-). Daughter of a Dublin preacher; wife, mother, and writer.

Patrick, Simon (1626-1707). A bishop and founder of schools, the Society for Promoting Christian Knowledge, and Society for the Propagation of the Gospel.

Patrick, St. (c. 390-c. 461). Itinerant preacher and teacher in Ireland; credited with having broken the power of heathenism in that country.

Persian liturgy, of Nestorians (6th century). Later branch of Syrian.

Pierpoint, Folliott Sandford (1835-1917). No information available.

Pilkington, James (c. 1520-1576). Bishop of Durham; supporter of the Reformation.

Polycarp, St. (c. 70-155/160). Bishop of Smyrna and martyr; knew eyewitnesses to the life of Christ.

Porete, Marguerite (?-1310). Member of the Beguine sisterhood who taught in northern France from the 1290s; her devotional works, long thought to be authored by an anonymous monk, were read in European monasteries and convents for over six centuries; she was burned to death for her ideas.

Pusey, Edward Bouverie (1800-1882). Leader of the Oxford Movement in the Church of England, which attempted to lead the church back into closer ties to the Roman Catholic Church.

Rauschenbusch, Walter (1861-1918). Baptist minister and educator; known for his strong views and written works on social change.

Richard, St. (1197-1253). Bishop of Chichester.

Ridley, Nicholas (c. 1500-1555). Reformer and bishop of London; helped compile Book of Common Prayer of 1549; burned at the stake for his beliefs.

Roman Breviary (various forms of the book, dated in different centuries). Book containing the psalms, hymns, and prayers used in the Roman worship service; usually printed in four volumes for the four seasons of the year; originally used primarily by those people serving in the choir.

Rossetti, Christina (1830-1894). Anglican poet; published several volumes.

Sailer, Johann Michael (1751-1832). Jesuit scholar.

Sarum Breviary (from 11th century). Medieval modification of the Roman Rite used at Salisbury, then in other diocese; it provided the main text for the first Book of Common Prayer.

Scougal, Henry (1650-1678). Scottish devotional writer.

Simeon Bar Sabbae (4th century). A bishop in Persia martyred in 339.

Slessor, Mary (1848-1915). Missionary to Calabar, Nigeria.

Solzhenitsyn, Aleksandr (1918-). Russian author and 1970 winner of the Nobel Prize.

Spurgeon, Charles Haddon (1834-1892). English Baptist preacher; founded college for training preachers, wrote Bible expositories, hymns, and sermons.

Stevenson, Robert Louis (1850-1894). Scottish poet and novelist.

Synesius of Cyrene (c. 370-c. 414). A bishop of Ptolemais in Cyrenaica.

Syrian liturgy, of Jacobites (from 5th century). See *Egyptian Rite.*

Tait, Archibald Campbell (1811-1882). Archbishop of Canterbury from 1868; his leadership helped restore Canterbury to a position of preeminence in Church of England.

Tauler, John (c. 1300-1361). German mystic who made the realm of mystical spirituality more accessible to ordinary believers, rather than just the spiritual "elite."

Taylor, Jeremy (1613-1667). Anglican bishop and writer, known for his poetic style.

Temple, William (1881-1944). Archbishop of Canterbury from 1942; writer, theologian, philosopher; concerned with social issues.

Teresa of Calcutta, Mother, (1910-). Albanian-born Indian nun and winner of the 1979 Nobel Prize; founder of the Missionaries of Charity.

Teresa of Avila, St. (1515-1582). Member of the Carmelite order; reformer, mystic, and writer.

Tersteegen, Gerhard (1697-1769). German hymnwriter and religious leader.

Therese of Lisieux, St. (1873-1897). Carmelite nun and devotional writer.

Thomas à Kempis (c. 1380-1471). German mystic, poet, devotional writer; famous for *The Imitation of Christ*.

Thurman, Howard (1900-1981). African American clergyman, scholar, and writer.

Tillotson, John (1630-1694). Archbishop of Canterbury from 1691; one of the most influential of English preachers.

Twells, Henry. No information available.

Underhill, Evelyn (1875-1941). Scholar of mysticism, writer.

Watts, Isaac (1674-1748). One of the most prolific and well-known hymnwriters.

Wesley, Charles (1707-1788). Evangelist, writer of over 7000 hymns; brother of John Wesley.

Wesley, John (1703-1791). Founder of Methodism; preacher and writer of sermons, treatises, translations.

Wesley, Susanna (1669-1742). Daughter of well-known Puritan minister, Dr. Samuel Annesley; "a woman of uncommon intelligence, beauty, charm, and strength of character"; mother of John and Charles Wesley.

Westcott, Brooke Foss (1825-1901). Theologian, scholar; helped with establishing New Testament from older manuscripts; also known for his commentaries.

Williams, Rowland (1817-1870). Religious writer.

Wilson, Thomas (1663-1755). Bishop and devotional writer.

Index